Bond

How to do ...
11+ Maths

Liz Heesom

 Nelson Thornes

Published in 2006 by:
Nelson Thornes Ltd
Delta Place
27 Bath Road
CHELTENHAM
GL53 7TH
United Kingdom

12 13 / 15 14 13 12

A catalogue record for this book is available from the British Library

ISBN 978 0 7487 9696 0

Editor: Nicola Morgan
Cover photograph: Jigsaw by Bananastock/Cadmium RF (NT)
Page make-up by GreenGate Publishing Services

Printed in China by 1010 Printing International Ltd

Contents

Standard 11+ Maths Test
(Central pull-out section)

Introduction

"Maths seems so difficult."

"I just can't seem to learn my tables."

"I can't understand fractions and decimals."

"My mind goes blank when I have a maths test to do."

Maths seems to be a subject about which many children can get anxious. This can be due to a lack of confidence, especially when so many new ways of learning mathematical concepts are introduced. Children have to use and respond to maths in many different ways during primary school and the 11+ exam can seem quite daunting if they are unsure about what they have to do.

The 11+/selective examinations system is still used to decide grammar and independent school entry in several parts of the UK. Depending on the requirements set by each Local Education Authority (LEA) and/or individual schools, children sitting the 11+ exam will complete one or more papers in the following subjects: maths, English, non-verbal reasoning and verbal reasoning. Your child's primary school should automatically inform you about these entrance exams once your child is in Year 5 but you can contact your LEA for more details before this.

The contents of this book are relevant to all children who are preparing for the maths paper for 11+/selective exams which they will take during their final year (Year 6) at primary school. *How to do 11+ Maths* can also be used as a key resource to support more general practice in maths.

① *What is an 11+ Maths exam?*

An 11+ Maths exam may differ from region to region, but a paper will generally require children to display:

- the ability to think and calculate quickly
- sound knowledge of tables
- the ability to apply the four number operations (+ − × ÷) accurately
- a fundamental understanding of number relationships, measurement, mental arithmetic, geometry and data handling

There are two different formats for 11+ Maths exam papers. Questions can either be presented in a **standard** or a **multiple-choice** layout. Standard is where a child writes his or her answers on the question paper. Multiple-choice is where possible answers are given on the paper and a child marks his or her chosen answer in a separate booklet.

The practice exercises in *How to do 11+ Maths* are written in a standard format, though the central pull-out test does include some multiple-choice tasks.

As with all exams, 11+ Maths papers are timed and they usually last from 45 minutes to one hour. Children therefore need to complete timed tests as well as working through non-timed practice, so they can see what they are able to do within a given time frame.

(2) How can you use this book?

How to do 11+ Maths is a practical guide designed for use by children, but it also has a wealth of essential advice and tips for adults involved in 11+ practice. The book works through the components that make up 11+ Maths papers, teaching and practising the skills needed to succeed in these exams. It tells children (and parents!) what to expect and provides sound strategies that can be practised and developed further.

It may not be necessary to work through all of the sections provided in this book because your child may already be quite confident in several areas. The quick test at the start of each section is designed to indicate whether your child already has a sound understanding of a topic or if he or she needs to work through the material in detail to reinforce what he or she knows or to learn new techniques. For example, topics such as cube numbers, square roots, equations and algebra may not have been covered in detail at school by the time your child starts practising for the 11+. By using the central pull-out test as a guide, you will also be able to see in which parts of 11+ Maths your child may need further practice.

How to do 11+ Maths is part of the well-known and long-established Bond series, whose finely-graded 11+ resources have been trusted by parents, teachers and tutors for over 40 years. This book accompanies the range of *Bond Assessment Papers in Maths*, which provide a variety of additional practice for 11+ Maths skills. The book can also be used to complement other general maths textbooks.

(3) How is this book organised?

This book is divided into sections which cover the topics most commonly tested in 11+ Maths papers. At school all children should learn the skills and content covered in this book and will be tested on all these elements at some stage, so each section is useful for general reference, practice and confidence-building.

There are three main sections to this book:

A Where do you start?

B The key 11+ Maths topics

C How do you prepare for the exam?

Section A provides clear guidance on the key knowledge and basic skills every child needs to have before starting more focused practice for 11+ Maths. It is important that you and your child find out which key skills you may need to practise together.

The tips in this section give essential advice on how to check and improve your child's basic mathematical skills.

Section B contains 27 separate topics, which are organised into five main subject groups: **Number**, **Fractions and decimals**, **Handling data**, **Shape and space** and **Measurement**. This section covers all the essential mathematical concepts your child needs to be familiar with in order to succeed at 11+ Maths. If your child scores well on an initial quick test, he or she should read through the **Key Facts** checklist found towards the end of each topic to reinforce any existing knowledge. It is recommended that your child completes the test in pencil. If they need to retake the test after working through the topic, they can then do so, filling in the second total box in order to compare their scores.

For those who need more support, topics provide:

- step-by-step explanations with worked examples
- practice activities – to be completed in this book:

  – to be completed in a notebook:
- helpful advice and hints for children and parents

Section C provides essential advice on exam technique and on preparing for the exam day itself.

The **central pull-out section** contains a full-length 11+ Maths practice paper. If you wish to set this as a 'before and after' test, please visit www.assessmentpapers.co.uk and follow the Free Resources link to download another free copy. The answers to the test are at the end of the main **Answers** section.

There is also a **glossary** towards the end of the book, which contains brief explanations of words or terms used in 11+ Maths.

To accompany this book, some **free electronic materials** are also available for you to download from our website at www.bond11plus.co.uk. You may find the **Maths Facts** cards of particular interest as these are a key learning tool that many children find fun and useful. Where other online materials relate to sections of this book, the following icon appears in the margin:

④ When should you start practising?

A good time to check up on basic skills is the summer term of Year 4. That gives you the summer holidays to:

Checklist

✓ practise and reinforce any knowledge or skills that are a little shaky
✓ consolidate tables and number bonds
✓ practise halving and doubling numbers
✓ become familiar with different types of measurement using activities such as cooking.

Once your child is settled into Year 5, it is important to establish a regular routine of practising tables – try to introduce a couple of quiet, uninterrupted sessions a week for practice.

By the autumn term of Year 5, you should be practising and reinforcing the different concepts outlined in this book. It is best to practise little and often, with an emphasis on quick thinking and rapid feedback. In 11+ Maths, children are expected to show dexterity in coping with numbers and the ability to solve problems of all kinds logically and with understanding. This would also be a good time to try the central pull-out test to see how your child copes with 11+ Maths tasks, as well as the maths Placement Test provided in *The Parents' Guide to the 11+*. (See inside cover for details.)

Remember that your child should be covering all the aspects of maths that he or she will need for the 11+ exam at school. Working to prepare for 11+ Maths outside school should therefore focus on highlighting particular difficulties, consolidating key skills and working to time. The *Bond Maths Assessment Papers* and *11+ Test Papers* give many opportunities to do this.

⑤ What do you need?

Checklist

✓ A stock of **pencils**, a good quality pencil sharpener and a supply of erasers.
✓ A clear plastic **30 cm ruler**.
✓ Wide-spaced, good quality lined **exercise books**, preferably stapled. It is a good idea to keep work in these so that your child can see the progress he or she has made and make a note of any facts that he or she needs to learn and practise.
✓ A small **kitchen timer** that can be used by your child for timed or speed work.
✓ A **calculator** for checking work.
✓ A simple geometry set consisting of **set squares** and a **protractor** in clear plastic and a **pair of compasses**.
✓ Access to **drinking water**.
✓ A **quiet, well-lit space** to work in.

A: Where do you start?

① Check basic skills

It is important to find out whether your child is capable of tackling 11+ Maths. Your child will need, above all, to have a clear knowledge and understanding of:

- number bonds to 20
- times tables facts
- place value
- doubling and halving numbers
- the four number operations
- units of measurement

Talk with your child's teacher and find out what he or she thinks. You may be able to find out your child's predicted mark for the Year 6 National Curriculum Test. (These are often still referred to as the SATs – Standard Assessment Tests.) At the end of Year 6, children aged about 11 are expected to achieve level 4 in English, maths and science.

If your child is already aged 10 or 11, you could try giving him or her the pull-out test from the middle of this book, to see how he or she performs on an 11+ style paper. This can be used as a 'before and after' 11+ practice test, if you download a free second copy from our website and time your child on both occasions. (The maths placement test found in *The Parents' Guide to the 11+* is also a useful gauge of your child's ability level. See inside cover for details.)

Whatever stage your child is at, you may find it useful to find out what he or she knows already and this will help to point towards things to practise before moving on to more focused 11+ practice. Here are some things to try out with your child:

- Count to 20 and back as quickly as possible.
- Say how many days in a week/each month/a year.
- Count forwards and backwards in 2s, 3s, 4s, 5s and 10s from different starting numbers.
- Sketch a range of shapes (e.g. quadrilaterals, triangles, regular and irregular shapes, etc.).
- Indicate $\frac{1}{2}$, $\frac{1}{4}$ and $\frac{3}{4}$ on these sketches by shading.
- Tell the time from analogue and digital clocks.
- Change 'quarter to' time to digital time.
- Indicate roughly what a centimetre and a metre look like and estimate measures.
- Read numbers up to 1 million, such as: 65; 3806; 70566.
- Practise multiplying and dividing by 10, for example: 781 × 10; 520 ÷ 10.
- Work out answers to a variety of calculations, in any way your child likes such as: 67 + 12; 71 – 37; 32 × 5; 57 ÷ 3.

 **PARENT TIP**

Try out these things casually, when your child is relaxed and keen to show what he or she knows. Weekends or holidays, when nothing else is going on, may be good moments.

The following sections cover the six basic skills, as mentioned above, which your child needs to know before beginning to work through the key 11+ Maths topics.

② Check number bonds to 20

It is vital that your child can quickly and easily add and subtract numbers with answers up to 20. These are known as the number bonds up to 20. Having a thorough knowledge of these will mean that more difficult numbers can also be added or subtracted quickly.

So, knowing that **7 + 8 = 15** makes it easy to work out that **17 + 8 = 25**.

Knowing that **19 – 15 = 4** makes it easy to work out that **29 – 15 = 14**.

The following activities can be used to help your child reinforce their knowledge of number bonds:

- Say a number between 1 and 19 and get your child to respond with the number that makes 20, or ask questions such as "20 take away what makes 11"
- Play card games such as *vingt-et-un* (also known as 'pontoon' or '21'), 'rummy' or 'uno', dice games such as Yahtzee, or number games such as darts, 'shut the box' or 'your number's up'.
- Spot patterns: 20 – 1 = 19; 20 – 2 = 18; 20 – 3 = 17, and so on.

 **PARENT TIP**

If your child has difficulty with any particular bonds, continue to practise them orally as well as making up short written tests focusing on those bonds.

③ Support times tables facts

Children may sometimes regard learning their times tables as a chore inflicted on them that has little relevance to anything else they do. In fact, children struggling with tables are likely to have related difficulties with:

- division
- fractions
- area
- volume
- prime numbers
- factors and multiples
- ratio and proportion
- percentages

Speed in calculating, understanding relationships between numbers, and confidence depend on recall of the times tables. For the purposes of 11+ Maths, it is helpful for children to know all times tables facts up to 12×12. It takes most children a lot of regular practice to learn times tables facts. Some children learn their tables by chanting them again and again, other children find it helpful to write them down. Help your child to find the method that works best for him or her.

Explain to your child the importance of learning tables. You can test your child's times tables facts knowledge with exercises such as the one below.

Using a stopwatch, get your child to count in twos to 24, in threes to 36, and so on as quickly as possible for the tables he or she feels comfortable with. Take it gently to begin with and give your child plenty of time to work out the answer.

✓ PARENT TIP

Keep a record of your child's personal best times for each times table to allow him or her to see these improving times. Some should be very quick, such as the times for the twos, fives and tens: quicker than five seconds is ideal. Any that take longer than 15 seconds need to be worked at and practised until they can be counted in less time.

Learning strategies

The seven, eight and nine times tables are often the most difficult for children to learn. Explain to your child that he or she will already know many of the facts from the easier times tables.

For example, facts such as:

2×7 5×8 10×9

will already be known from the two, five and ten times tables. This can make the learning seem less daunting.

To begin with your child may find it easiest to count on or back from known facts to work out the answer for unknown facts (count on seven from $7 \times 5 = 35$ to work out 7×6 or back seven for 7×4). The more he or she practises, the more familiar the facts will become and he or she will remember them without needing to count.

Using these suggestions can help your child remember facts:

- **Rhyme:** six fours are twenty-four, six sixes are thirty-six, six eights are forty-eight.
- **Humour:** 'She ate and she ate 'til she was sick on the floor.' for 'Eight eights are sixty-four.'
- **Pattern:** $7 \times 8 = 56$, notice how the digits put in order are 5, 6, 7, 8. Many of the tables have patterns in the sequence of answers.
- **Doubling and halving:** $4 \times 7 = 28$ and therefore 8×7 will be double 28, which equals 56. $10 \times 7 = 70$ and therefore 5×7 will be half of 70, which equals 35.
- **Visual:** write difficult facts onto a piece of card with a vertical folded flap hiding the answer, or onto sticky notes stuck around the house with the answer written on the back.

When your child has learnt to count quickly and accurately in all the tables up to 12, the next stage is for him or her to practise the facts all jumbled up. It is helpful to do a regular tables test, perhaps once a week, using the tables tests found on our website or by asking your child 20 facts. Gradually reduce the amount of time you give your child to answer questions.

Division and times tables

By the end of Year 5, your child should know the facts in all the tables, including related facts. So, for **7 × 4 = 28**, he or she should also know:

$$4 \times 7 = 28 \qquad 28 \div 4 = 7 \qquad 28 \div 7 = 4$$

Practise regularly with your child: on the way to school, in the car, whenever you have a quiet moment. For instance, for the seven times table (one many children find hard to learn) ask questions using both multiplication and division:

7 times 6?

How many 7s in 70?

How many 7s in 21?

7 times 12?

More useful tables skills

Once your child knows his or her times tables up to 12 × 12, then it is fairly easy to work out times tables that are multiples of 10:

20 × is the same as multiplying by 2 followed by 10.

30 × is the same as multiplying by 3 followed by 10.

40 × is the same as multiplying by 4 followed by 10, and so on.

Knowing the 25 times and 250 times tables is extremely useful for dealing with units of measurement. See how quickly your child can jot down multiples of 25 up to 500, spotting the patterns, and then multiples of 250 up to 2500. Listen to him or her practise counting in 25s and 250s.

(4) Help your child with place value

Your child needs to understand how our number system works and how the value of a number depends on where it is placed. He or she must be able to read numbers up to a million correctly and to be able to multiply or divide any given whole number by 10 quickly. It is also important that your child is able to read a decimal number correctly, and to understand what the numbers after the decimal point mean.

To check your child's knowledge of place value, ask him or her to complete tasks such as:

- reading aloud a range of whole numbers, e.g. 29; 687; 2905; 45 174; 360 512
- multiplying a given number by 10, e.g. 687
- dividing a given number by 10, e.g. 450
- reading aloud a range of decimal numbers, e.g. 7.6; 35.02; 514.89; 0.56

PARENT TIP

Many children read the decimal point incorrectly as 'dot' rather than 'point' and the numbers after the decimal point, for instance in 514.89, as 'eighty-nine' rather than 'eight, nine'.

If your child wants to write down a calculation, inserts a zero in the middle, doesn't know the answers, then go to topic 1: Place value (p. 8) for further place value practice.

⑤ *Help your child with doubling and halving*

By the end of Year 5, your child should be able to double all numbers up to 50 quickly and correctly. He or she also needs to be able to halve numbers, including odd numbers, up to 100 and beyond.

Give your child numbers to double and halve. He or she will have to use strategies like doubling or halving the 10s first and then the units; familiarity will improve speed. It is useful to begin with the 10s numbers first. So, for example, try asking them to:

- double 30, halve 90, double 40, halve 50
- double multiples of 5 or even numbers
- halve even numbers
- double numbers like 37 or 49

Next give your child odd numbers to halve. For these it is helpful for him or her to find half of the even number that precedes it and add on $\frac{1}{2}$.

So, for half of 77: **76 ÷ 2 = 38** and then **38 + $\frac{1}{2}$ = 38$\frac{1}{2}$ = 38.5.**

These doubling and halving sequences are extremely useful for your child to know and recognise:

1, 2, 4, 8, 16, 32, 64, 128, 256, 512, 1024, 2048...

..., 2048, 1024, 512, 256, 128, 64, 32, 16, 8, 4, 2, 1

If your child is familiar with these numbers, he or she can quickly work out the answers to calculations such as **£2.56 ÷ 4** by halving, then halving again, or 128 × 8 by doubling, doubling, then doubling:

£2.56 $\xrightarrow{\text{halve}}$ £1.28 $\xrightarrow{\text{halve}}$ £0.64   128 $\xrightarrow{\text{double}}$ 256 $\xrightarrow{\text{double}}$ 512 $\xrightarrow{\text{double}}$ 1024

⑥ Revise the four number operations

Your child must know vocabulary associated with each of the four number operations:

$$+ \quad - \quad \times \quad \div$$

These are provided in topics 2 and 3 of Section B (pp. 11–17). Your child will need frequent reminding and practice until he or she can confidently identify which number operation is required when he or she comes across one of the words in a problem.

✔ PARENT TIP

It is useful to have a sticky note divided into four sections onto which your child can write the different vocabulary for each of the operations. The note can then be moved to whatever work is being done.

Your child also needs to know that + or – and × or ÷ are inverse (opposite) operations and that when working with whole numbers (integers), + or × make numbers larger, while – or ÷ make numbers smaller.

The symbols for 'greater than' and 'less than' can be easily confused with each other but it is important for your child to identify which is which:

✔ PARENT TIP

Help your child to remember that the arrowhead ALWAYS points to the smaller number!

    < means 'is less than' or 'is smaller than', so 4 < 6

    > means 'is greater than' or 'is larger than', so 8 > 3

Try using varied language for the = sign so your child fully understands its meaning:

| equals | is the same as | balances | has the same value as | makes |

⑦ Check units of measurement

It is important for your child to be familiar with both metric and imperial units of measurement for 11+ Maths. Topic 25: Metric and imperial units of measurement (p. 88) provides metric equivalences together with approximate equivalences between metric and imperial units of measurement.

There are also suggestions of everyday items measuring certain lengths, weights and capacities to help your child visualise different units of measurement. However, the best way for your child to understand measures is for him or her to have practical opportunities to estimate and then measure items him- or herself. Try to create a variety of opportunities when at home and out and about.

✔ PARENT TIP

Help your child to look for familiar parts of other mathematical words to help him or her remember equivalences, for example:
*cent-: centimetre (**100** in a metre), century (**100** years).*
*milli-: millimetre, milligram, millilitre (**1000** in a metre/gram/litre).*
*kilo-: kilometre, kilogram (**1000** metres/grams).*

B: The key 11+ Maths topics

Maths at 11+ or entrance exam level can seem quite challenging. This section of the book aims to help you work through the topics that most children find confusing. It will also help you find ways of answering questions that you understand!

If you are in Year 5 or 6, first try the pull-out test from the centre of this book to test yourself under exam conditions. It will help you to see which questions you find the most difficult and those will be the ones to spend the most time practising.

The key 11+ Maths topics covered in this section are:

- Number
- Fractions and decimals
- Handling data
- Shape and space
- Measurement

REMEMBER!

Key words that you need to know will be explained in the relevant sections but you can also use the glossary at the back for explanations of mathematical terms.

At the beginning of each topic there is a short test. Complete the test and then mark it, giving yourself one point for each correct answer. If you get nine or more answers correct, then you can move on to the next topic after reading the **Key Facts** checklist at the end of the topic. If you get eight answers or fewer correct, then you need to work through that topic step-by-step, attempt the practice activities and then retake the test before moving on.

"I get so confused with maths."

The two most common reasons for getting questions wrong in maths are:

- **not reading the question correctly** or
- **making silly mistakes**

Everyone makes these kinds of mistakes. You must read each question and think about it carefully, using all the clues in the words or diagrams to help you. When you have an answer, check it carefully to avoid making a careless mistake.

"There seem to be so many different ways of doing things."

You're right; there are many different ways of doing things in maths. Everyone is different and our brains work in different ways. Your job is to find what works for you. This takes practice and persistence!

For example, to work out £1.26 × 8 you could use any of these ways to calculate the answer:

○	**multiply:**	£1.26
		× 8
		£10.08
○	**split:**	£1.26 = £1.00 + £0.20 + £0.06
	then multiply:	£1.00 × 8 = £8.00, £0.20 × 8 = £1.60, £0.06 × 8 = £0.48
	then add:	£8.00 + £1.60 + £0.48 = **£10.08**
○	**double, double and double:** £1.26 ⟶ £2.52 ⟶ £5.04 ⟶ **£10.08**

So, when you next feel confused by the best way to work out an answer, use the way that makes the most sense to you. It may not be the method your teachers suggest; it may be a different way from how your friends or parents work it out, but if it makes sense to you, and it gives you the correct answer, then don't be afraid to follow the technique you feel the most comfortable using. The practice activities in each section will help you practise different techniques.

Remember, whichever techniques you use, you must make sure you work quickly and accurately. If your answer is just one number out or a decimal point is in the wrong place, your answer will be incorrect.

Number

① Place value

Try this test to find out how much you already know about place value.

1	Multiply 60 by 300. _____	1
2	Divide 305 by 1000. _____	1
3	Round 73 071 to the nearest 100. _____	1
4	How many times must you subtract 0.03 from 3 to reach 0? _____	1
5	How many thousands equal 50 hundreds? _____	1

6 What are the values of the 3 marked with an *x* and the 3 marked with a *y*?

    x *y*
43.93 _____ | 1

7 Circle the 6 worth 6 hundreds: 66 666. | 1

8 Round 685 to the nearest 100. _____ | 1

9 Round 8345 to the nearest 1000. _____ | 1

10 How many is 1.55 to the nearest tenth? _____ | 1

| 10 TOTAL | | 10 TOTAL |

How did you do?

○ Nine or ten correct? Read the **Key Facts** and then go on to topic 2: Addition and subtraction problems.

○ Eight or fewer correct? Work through this topic carefully and then retake the test!

Knowing the value of digits

You need to know the value of a digit wherever it appears in a number.

Multiplying and dividing by 10, 100, 1000

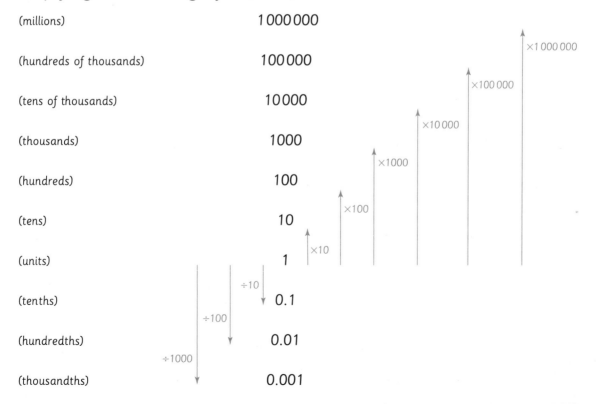

(millions)	1 000 000
(hundreds of thousands)	100 000
(tens of thousands)	10 000
(thousands)	1000
(hundreds)	100
(tens)	10
(units)	1
(tenths)	0.1
(hundredths)	0.01
(thousandths)	0.001

×10   ×100   ×1000   ×10 000   ×100 000   ×1 000 000

÷10   ÷100   ÷1000

Fill in the missing numbers.

When a number is **multiplied** by:

- **10**, all digits move **one** column to the **left**. One zero is needed; in the units column.
- **100**, all digits move **two** columns to the **left**. _____ zeros are needed; one in the units column and one in the tens column.
- **1000**, all digits move _____ columns to the _____. _____ zeros are needed; one in the units column, one in the tens column and one in the hundreds column.

When a number is **divided** by:

- **10**, all digits move **one** column to the **right**.
- **100**, all digits move two columns to the **right**.
- **1000**, all digits move _____ columns to the _____.

Now it's your turn!

Divide 8 million by 10 repeatedly. Watch how the numbers move!

"What about decimal numbers?"

As with whole numbers, when you use decimal numbers all digits in the number have to move in one direction and the same number of columns. Just remember to keep the digits in the same order!

$$147.5 \div 100 = 1.475$$

"What about numbers with no decimal point?"

Whole numbers can be written with a decimal point but must have one or more zeros in the columns representing tenths, hundredths, and so on:

$$73 = 73.0 = 73.0000000 \ldots$$

Rounding numbers

Rounding a number to the nearest 10, 100, 1000, 10 000 means finding the nearest multiple of 10, 100, 1000, 10 000 to that number. You can round up or round down. Rounding up means finding the next largest multiple of your rounding number. Rounding down means finding the next smallest multiple of your rounding number. So, if you are rounding to the nearest 10, you go up or down to the next multiple of 10.

Look at this example:

Round **12 094** to the nearest **100**.

12 094
↑

The digit in the tens column is **greater than five** so round **up** to the next multiple of 100.

12 094 rounded to the nearest 100 is **12 100**.

REMEMBER!

Look at the number in the column to the **right** of the one you are asked to round to. If it is **less than five**, round down. If it is **five or greater than five**, round up.

The same idea works for decimals, so you can round off to a certain number of decimal places. To decide whether you must round up or down, look at the digit to the right of the decimal place to which you need to round.

For example:

12.264 rounded to **one** decimal place (the nearest tenth) is **12.3**.

12.264 rounded to **two** decimal places (the nearest hundredth) is **12.26**.

Now it's your turn!

1 Round 345 678 to the nearest:

10 _____   100 _____

1000 _____   10 000 _____

2 Round 476.528 to the nearest:

tenth _____   hundredth: _____

✔ PARENT TIP

Look out for how different numbers are written in newspapers or magazines. Help your child to read them and discuss how they would change if they were rounded up or down to the nearest 10, 100, 1000, etc.

KEY FACTS

- The digits to the left of the decimal point show the number of units, tens, hundreds and thousands, and so on. The digits to the right of the decimal point show the number of tenths, hundredths, thousandths, and so on.

- To **multiply** by 10, 100 or 1000, move the digits to the **left** to make them larger.

- To **divide** by 10, 100 or 1000, move the digits to the **right** to make them smaller.

- If the digit in the column to the **right** of the one you are asked to round to is **less than five**, round down. If it is **five or greater than five**, round up.

② *Addition and subtraction problems*

Try this test to find out how much you already know about addition and subtraction problems.

1–2	789 + 532 = _____ 5001 − 356 = _____	**2**
3	The Empire State Building is 381 m high. Ben Nevis is 1343 m high. How much higher is Ben Nevis than the Empire State Building? _____	**1**

4 In a library there were 158 fiction books and 132 non-fiction books. How many books is this short of the total of 350 books that there should be in the library?

_____   [ ] 1

5 How much less than 747 is 474? _____   [ ] 1

6 34 + 5 = 6 + 8 + _____   [ ] 1

7 Decrease £5.65 by £1.99. _____   [ ] 1

8 Increase £7.99 by £2.50. _____   [ ] 1

9 Find the sum of 1786 and 2965. _____   [ ] 1

10 What is the difference between 1786 and 2965? _____   [ ] 1

[ ] 10 TOTAL [ ] 10 TOTAL

How did you do?
- Nine or ten correct? Read the **Key Facts** and then go on to topic 3: Multiplication and division problems.
- Eight or fewer correct? Work through this topic carefully and then retake the test!

"I never know whether I'm supposed to be adding or subtracting."

Addition

An easy way to identify problems that can be solved using addition is by looking out for these words, phrases and symbols – they all mean 'add':

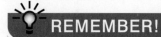

+   how many altogether   find the sum   plus   add   increase   find the total

Adding a whole number onto another number gives an answer **larger** than the number you started with.

To add on in your head, it can be helpful to start with the larger number and add on the smaller number or numbers in easy jumps. Remember the jumps as you go and then add the jumps together.

It can be helpful to write the numbers one under the other to ensure you add together the digits in their columns:

For example:

```
  1 3 2 2
  2 4 8 3
+ 5 2 1 9
  8 0 0 0   Total the thousands
    9 0 0   Total the hundreds
    1 1 0   Total the tens
      1 4   Total the units
  9 0 2 4   The grand total!
```

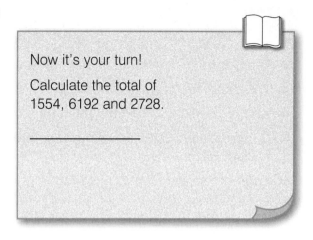

Now it's your turn!

Calculate the total of 1554, 6192 and 2728.

_____

Subtraction

An easy way to identify problems that can be solved using subtraction is by looking out for these words, phrases and symbols – they all mean 'subtract':

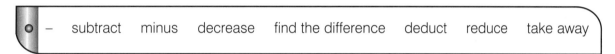

–   subtract   minus   decrease   find the difference   deduct   reduce   take away

Subtracting a positive number from another number gives an answer **smaller** than the number you started with. Usually at 11+ stage you subtract the smaller number from the larger number.

To subtract in your head, it can be helpful to start from the smaller number and count up to the larger number in easy jumps. Remember the jumps as you go and then add the jumps together.

Finding the difference between two numbers means the smaller number must be subtracted from the larger number. Alternatively you can count on from the smaller number to the larger number:

```
    8 4 3
  − 3 8 7
      1 3   to make 400
    4 4 3   to make 843
    4 5 6
```

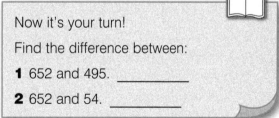

Now it's your turn!

Find the difference between:

1 652 and 495. _____

2 652 and 54. _____

Addition and subtraction involving money

Rounding up to the next pound can make calculations involving money much easier to work out in your head. For example:

99p is nearly £1   £1.99 is nearly £2   £7.99 is nearly £8

But, remember to adjust your answer to deal with the penny difference!

- The **opposite** or **inverse** of addition is subtraction.
- The **opposite** or **inverse** of subtraction is addition.
- **Add** is the same as **find the total, plus, increase, find the sum, how many altogether**.
- **Subtract** is the same as **take away, minus, find the difference, decrease, reduce, deduct**.
- **Estimate** answers (make a **sensible guess**) before you work out the actual answer.

 PARENT TIP

Encourage your child to use his or her skills in everyday situations. For example, when you're shopping, ask your child to work out the cost of a few items or to say how much change you will receive.

③ *Multiplication and division problems*

Try this test to find out how much you already know about multiplication and division problems.

1 $4 \times 2 \times \underline{\hspace{1.5cm}} = 160$ 1

2 Find the cost of 6 books that each cost £6.95. $\underline{\hspace{3cm}}$ 1

3 Multiply 630 by 55. $\underline{\hspace{2.5cm}}$ 1

4 How many 31p stamps can you buy for £6.20? $\underline{\hspace{1.5cm}}$ 1

5 What would 6 pens cost if 11 pens cost £7.48? $\underline{\hspace{2.5cm}}$ 1

6 The product of two numbers is 168. If one of the numbers is 24, what is the other?

$\underline{\hspace{2.5cm}}$ 1

7 How many 125 g packets can be filled from a drum containing 5 kg?

$\underline{\hspace{2.5cm}}$ 1

8 1 litre 800 ml × 5 = $\underline{\hspace{2cm}}$ ml   1

9 Circle the quotient for this division calculation: 6300 ÷ 70:

90   19   29   9   900

□ 1

10 What is the smallest number divisible by 2, 3 and 4? _____

□ 1

□ 10 TOTAL   ■ 10 TOTAL

How did you do?

○ Nine or ten correct? Read the **Key Facts** and then go on to topic 4: Mixed or several-step problems.

○ Eight or fewer correct? Work through this topic carefully and then retake the test!

"I'm never sure whether to multiply or to divide."

Multiplication

An easy way to identify problems that can be solved using multiplication is by looking out for these word, phrases and symbols – they all mean 'multiply':

○ ×   multiply   times   find the product

Multiplying a number by a positive integer (whole number) gives an answer **larger** than the number you started with.

A multiplication grid can be drawn quickly and helps to break down difficult multiplication questions such as **326 × 42**:

×	300	20	6
40	12 000	800	240
2	600	40	12

```
  12 000           600
+    800     +      40          13 040
+    240     +      12      +      652
   13 040           652          13 692
```

Now it's your turn!

Find the total weight of 72 boxes weighing 198 kg each.

Division

An easy way to identify problems that can be solved using division is by looking out for these, phrases and symbols – they all mean 'divide':

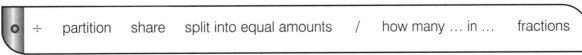

○ ÷   partition   share   split into equal amounts   /   how many ... in ...   fractions

Dividing a number by a positive integer (whole number) gives an answer **smaller** than the number you started with.

A number is **divisible** by a smaller number if the smaller number divides **exactly** into the larger number. So, 25 is divisible by 5 because 5 divides into 25 exactly.

REMEMBER!

The number you get when you divide one number by another is called a **quotient**.

This list of quick ways to test the divisibility of a number is very useful to learn.

A number is divisible by or a multiple of:
- 2 if it is even
- 3 if the sum of the digits is divisible by 3
- 4 if the last two digits are a number divisible by 4
- 5 if the units digit is 5 or 0
- 6 if the number is even and divisible by 3
- 9 if the sum of the digits is divisible by 9
- 10 if the units digit is 0

✓ PARENT TIP

Use every opportunity to show your child practical ways of applying their multiplication and division skills, for example when calculating the total cost of several of the same item, when sharing out pocket money, etc.

(See topic 5: Factors and multiples, p. 19, to learn about multiples.)

You can **divide** by using **repeated subtraction**, taking the same amount away again and again until there is nothing left, or there is a smaller remainder. Your answer is the number of times you were able to subtract the amount, with the remainder if there is one.

REMEMBER!

The remainder is sometimes very important. For example, you might need to work out how many coaches are needed to take children on a school trip. If there are children remaining after coaches have been completely filled, then an extra coach will still be needed to take them on their trip!

Look at this example:

How many pencils costing 30p each can be bought for £8.00?

```
   £8.00
 – £3.00    10 × 30p
   £5.00
 – £3.00    10 × 30p
   £2.00
 – £1.50     5 × 30p
   £0.50
 – £0.30     1 × 30p
   £0.20
```

Now it's your turn!

In Grove Primary School, the maximum number of children they can have in a class is 32. How many classes will they need for 653 children? _____

10 + 10 + 5 + 1 = 26 pencils costing 30p each can be bought for £8.00 with 20p left over. The remainder (20p) is not enough to buy another pencil.

- The opposite or **inverse** of multiplication is division.
- The opposite or **inverse** of division is multiplication.
- Multiply is the same as **find the product**, **times**, **groups** or **lots of**.
- Divide is the same as **share** or **split into equal amounts**, **partition** or **fractions**. You can say **"How many … in …?"** to help yourself.
- A number is **divisible by** a smaller number if the smaller number divides **exactly** into the larger number.
- The answer in a division calculation is the **quotient**.

(4) Mixed or several-step problems

Try this test to find out how much you already know about mixed or several-step problems.

1 Rosie bought 5 metres of curtain material. She gave the shop assistant £20 and received £1.75 change. How much did the material cost per metre? _____ | 1 |

2 Jack had 170 stickers. He put 18 on each of 9 pages in his sticker album. How many stickers did he have left over? _____ | 1 |

3 There were 2.5 litres of squash for 4 children. 100 ml got spilt and the rest was divided equally between the children. How much did each child get in ml? _____ | 1 |

4 A village school of 57 children has 1 class of 11 children. The rest are divided into 2 equal classes. How many children are in each of these 2 classes? _____ | 1 |

5 Find the difference in grams between one half of a kilogram and eight tenths of a kilogram. _____ | 1 |

6 100 packs of butter, each with a mass of 65 g, are packed into a box. The box has a mass of 400 g left unfilled. Find the total mass of the full box in kilograms. _____ | 1 |

7 Samir cuts 1.64 m and then a further 2.09 m from a 4 m length of wood. How much of the wood is left in metres? _____ | 1 |

8 How much change from £10 does Sharee have if she buys a book for £4.25 and a pen for £2.95? _____ `1`

9 Emily multiplied a number by 7 instead of dividing it by 7. Her answer was 5145. What should her answer have been? _____ `1`

10 Todd bought 14 toys for £1.35 each and sold them each for £1.70. How much was the total profit that he made? _____ `1`

`10` TOTAL `10` TOTAL

How did you do?

- Nine or ten correct? Read the **Key Facts** and then go on to topic 5: Factors and multiples.
- Eight or fewer correct? Work through this topic carefully and then retake the test!

"I never know what to do first with problems."

Problem-solving steps

Problems are often made up of many stages and you will need several different operations in order to find the answers. Following a clear set of steps, such as the '6-point plan' below, could make problems easier to work out.

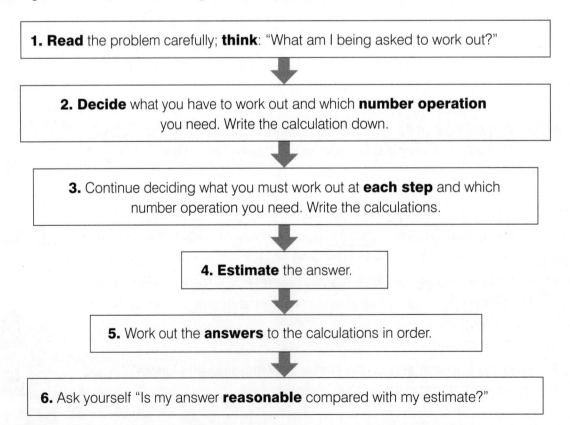

1. **Read** the problem carefully; **think**: "What am I being asked to work out?"

2. **Decide** what you have to work out and which **number operation** you need. Write the calculation down.

3. Continue deciding what you must work out at **each step** and which number operation you need. Write the calculations.

4. **Estimate** the answer.

5. Work out the **answers** to the calculations in order.

6. Ask yourself "Is my answer **reasonable** compared with my estimate?"

Now it's your turn!

Mrs Ellis needs to buy enough exercise books for three classes of children.

Two classes have 27 children and the third class has 29 children in it. Each child needs two exercise books.

How many books does Mrs Ellis need to buy? Work through the question in your notebook and then write the answer here.

_____

KEY FACTS

- There are four number operations: +, −, × and ÷. Look again at topics 2 and 3 to remind yourself of the different mathematical words used to mean add, subtract, multiply and divide.

- Try following the 6-point plan to help decide what you are being asked to do in a several-step problem.

- **Profit** means how much extra money you can earn if you sell something for more than it cost.

✓ PARENT TIP

When shopping, ask your child to calculate the amount of change you will receive from a given amount of money when buying several items. Your child should then realise that he or she must work out the total cost before being able to work out how much change you will be given.

⑤ Factors and multiples

Try this test to find out how much you already know about factors and multiples.

1 Write down all the numbers between 30 and 70 that are exactly divisible by 8.

_____ | 1 |

2 Which is the smallest number that is a multiple of both 4 and 6? ____ | 1 |

3 Circle the numbers that are factors of both 48 and 72:

4,   6,   8,   9,   63 | 1 |

4 Find all the factors of 48. _____ | 1 |

5 Which multiples of 7 are greater than 60 and less than 90?

_____ | 1 |

6 What is the highest common factor of 32, 88 and 120? _____ | 1 |

7 Find the lowest common multiple of 10, 12 and 15. _____ | 1 |

8 Circle the prime factors of 77:   6,   7,   8,   9,   10,   11 | 1 |

9 Express the number 36 in prime factors. _____ | 1 |

10 Circle the number that is a multiple of 13, has a prime number between
4 and 8 as a factor and has digits that add up to 10:
37,   46,   55,   64,   73,   82,   91 | 1 |

| 10 | | 10 |
| TOTAL | | TOTAL |

How did you do?
- Nine or ten correct? Read the **Key Facts** and then go on to topic 6: Special numbers.
- Eight or fewer correct? Work through this topic carefully and then retake the test!

Factors

An easy way to be sure of finding all the factors in a
number is to find them in pairs like this:

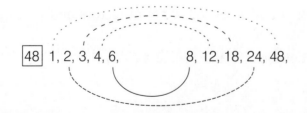

48 1, 2, 3, 4, 6,   8, 12, 18, 24, 48,

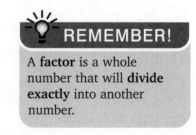

REMEMBER!

A **factor** is a whole
number that will **divide
exactly** into another
number.

You may have to find the **highest common factor (HCF)** of a set of numbers. To do
this, find all the factors of the numbers you are given and see which factors they have
in common or share. The largest one is the highest common factor.

Look at this example:

Find the HCF of 24, 42 and 48.

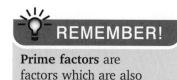

The factors of 24 are: 1, 2, 3, 4, **6**, 8, 12, 24.

The factors of 42 are: 1, 2, 3, **6**, 7, 14, 21, 42.

The factors of 48 are: 1, 2, 3, 4, **6**, 8, 12, 16, 24, 48.

The HCF of 24, 42 and 48 is **6**.

Now it's your turn!

Find the HCF of 21, 35 and 56.

_____

_____

_____

The HCF of 21, 35 and 56 is _____.

(To remind yourself about prime numbers turn to page 24.)

Multiples

A **multiple** of a number is the answer when it is multiplied by another number. $4 \times 5 = 20$. 20 is a multiple of 4 and 5.
The multiples of 5 are 5, 10, 15, 20, 25, etc.

You may have to find the **lowest common multiple (LCM)** of a set of numbers. To do this, write down the first five multiples of the highest number. Check to see if one of these is a multiple of all of the other numbers. If it's not in the first five, try the next five until you find the LCM.

Look at this example:

Find the LCM of 4, 6 and 9.

The first nine multiples of 4: 4,   8,   12,   16,   20,   24,   28,   32,   **36**

The first six multiples of 6:   6,   12,   18,   26,   30,   **36**

The first five multiples of 9:   9,   18,   27,   **36**,   45

The LCM of 4, 6 and 9 is 36.

Now it's your turn!

Find the LCM of 3, 8 and 12.

_____

_____

_____

The LCM of 3, 8 and 12 is _____ .

✓ PARENT TIP

Children frequently get maths words like 'factors' and 'multiples' muddled up. Using these words when practising times tables can help children to remember their meanings.

KEY FACTS

- A **factor** is a whole number that will **divide exactly** into another number.
- The **HCF** (highest common factor) of a set of numbers is the largest number that is a factor of all numbers in the set.
- The **prime factors** of a number are the prime numbers which can be multiplied together to make that number.
- A **multiple** of a number is the answer when the number is multiplied by another number.
- The **LCM** (lowest common multiple) of a set of numbers is the smallest number that is a multiple of all numbers in the set.

⑥ *Special numbers*

Try this test to find out how much you already know about special numbers.

1 On New Year's Day the temperature in the garden was –5°C. Inside the shed, it was 8°C. How much warmer was it in the shed than outside in the garden?

_____

☐ 1

2 $3^2 + 5^2 = $ _____

☐ 1

3 How many degrees below zero is –34°C? _____

☐ 1

4 Write 7×7 in index form. _____

☐ 1

5 Work out 5^3. _____ [1]

6 $\sqrt{64} + \sqrt{9} =$ _____ [1]

7 Circle the prime numbers:

40 41 42 43 44 45 46 47 48 49 [1]

8 Work out the answer to this calculation and write your answer in Roman numerals.

VI + IV = _____ [1]

9 Find three consecutive numbers that add up to 42. _____ [1]

10 Which triangular number is the same as $\sqrt{81}$ added to 2^2 added to the prime number between 20 and 28? _____ [1]

10 TOTAL   10 TOTAL

How did you do?
- Nine or ten correct? Read the **Key Facts** and then go on to topic 7: Sequences.
- Eight or fewer correct? Work through this topic carefully and then retake the test!

There are some particular types of numbers that you need to be able to recognise for 11+ Maths. A short section on each of the eight main types is given below.

Negative numbers

On a number line positive numbers are to the right of 0 and are larger than 0.
Negative numbers are to the left of 0 and are smaller than 0:

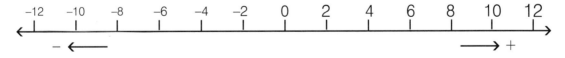

Imagine the zero in front of you and the **positive** numbers trailing off towards the right, getting larger, and the **negative** numbers trailing off towards the left, getting smaller.

A thermometer shows positive and negative numbers on a vertical scale. Freezing point is zero. Above zero are positive numbers. Below zero are negative numbers.

Square numbers

The first twelve **square numbers** are:

1, 4, 9, 16, 25, 36, 49, 64, 81, 100, 121, 144.

4^2 means 'four **squared**'. The small number (the index number) tells you that you must multiply **4** by itself.

$1 \times 1 = 1^2 = 1$

$2 \times 2 = 2^2 = 4$

$3 \times 3 = 3^2 = 9$

$4 \times 4 = 4^2 = 16...$

Cube numbers

The first six **cube numbers** are: **1, 8, 27, 64, 125, 216.**

4^3 means 'four **cubed**'. The small number tells you that you must multiply **4** by itself then multiply the answer by **4**.

$1 \times 1 \times 1 = 1^3 = 1$

$2 \times 2 \times 2 = 2^3 = 8$

$3 \times 3 \times 3 = 3^3 = 27$

$4 \times 4 \times 4 = 4^3 = 64...$

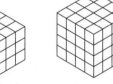

1 × 1 × 1   2 × 2 × 2   3 × 3 × 3   4 × 4 × 4

When a cube is built using centimetre cubes, starting with just one cube for the first cube, the number of cubes used to make the increasingly large cubes is the same as the cubed numbers.

Consecutive numbers

Consecutive numbers are numbers that follow on in order. So a set of numbers such as **45, 46, 47, 48, 49, 50** is consecutive. A group of numbers like **46, 45, 47, 50, 49** is not consecutive.

Prime numbers

The first 10 **prime numbers** are all less than 30:

2, 3, 5, 7, 11, 13, 17, 19, 23, 29

1 is not a prime number because it has only one factor: 1
2 is the only even prime number! Can you see why?

Roman numerals

Here are seven **Roman numerals** and their standard number values:

Roman	I	V	X	L	C	D	M
Standard	1	5	10	50	100	500	1000

Notice that the roman numeral X (10) is made up of a V and another upside-down V (5):

V + V = X   (5 + 5 = 10)

You can make up any other whole number by using a combination of these seven roman numerals. For example:

XIII = 13   (10 + 3)   DXI = 511   (500 + 10 + 1)

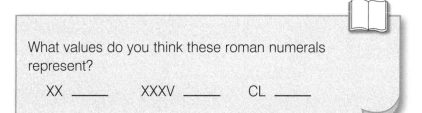

What values do you think these roman numerals represent?

XX ____   XXXV ____   CL ____

REMEMBER!

Dates are sometimes written using roman numerals:
MMVI = 2006

You may also need to know the value of these Roman numerals:

XL = 40   LX = 60   XC = 90

Triangular numbers

If you arrange dots in a triangular pattern, then the increasing number of dots needed to make a triangle form the sequence of **triangular numbers**.

These are the first 10 triangular numbers:

1, 3, 6, 10, 15, 21, 28, 36, 45, 55

The difference between each pair of numbers goes up by 1 each time. The first difference is 2, then 3, then 4, and so on.

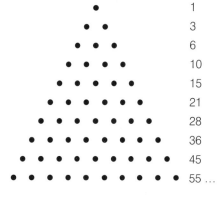

Square root

The square root of a number is the number you multiply by itself to make that number. The square root of 100 is 10 because 10 × 10 is 100. The square root of 49 is 7 because 7 × 7 is 49.

The symbol for a square root is: $\sqrt{}$. So, the square root of 49 is written as $\sqrt{49}$.

1 Add 4 squared to the fifth triangle number.

2 Subtract the square root of 49 from 5 cubed.

KEY FACTS

- **Negative numbers** are less than zero: –1, –2, –3…
- **Square numbers** multiply a number by itself: (1 × 1, 2 × 2, 3 × 3…)
- **Cube numbers** multiply a number by itself twice: (1 × 1 × 1, 2 × 2 × 2, 3 × 3 × 3…)
- **Consecutive numbers** follow on in order: 21, 22, 23
- **Prime numbers** have only two factors (1 and the number itself): 2, 3, 5, 7
- **Roman numerals:** letters represent numbers
  V = 5, X = 10, L = 50, C = 100, D = 500, M = 1000
  (see page 25 for more examples)
- **Triangular numbers:** 1, 3, 6, 10, 15
- **The square root** is the number you multiply by itself to make a larger number.

> ✔ **PARENT TIP**
>
> *Encourage your child to look out for these types of numbers so he or she can become familiar with them. For instance, Roman numerals are often seen on clock faces; negative numbers on thermometers and weather forecasts!*

---

⑦ Sequences

Try this test to find out how much you already know about sequences.

Complete the following sequences:

1 $3\frac{1}{2}$, $4\frac{1}{4}$,   5, $5\frac{3}{4}$,   _____   ☐ 1

2   100,   90,   _____,   73,   66   ☐ 1

3   47,   52,   58,   65,   _____   ☐ 1

4   2,   5,   11,   20,   _____   ☐ 1

5   2,   4,   8,   _____,   32,   64   ☐ 1

| 6 | 1, | 2, | 3, | 4, | 5, | 8, | 7, | 16, | ____ | | 1 |

| 7 | 1, | $1\frac{1}{2}$, | $2\frac{1}{2}$, | 4, | ____ | | 1 |

| 8 | 0.125, | 0.25, | 0.375, | 0.5 | ____ | | 1 |

| 9 | 10 000, | 1000, | 100, | ____, | 1, | 0.1, | 0.01 | | 1 |

| 10 | 1, | 3, | 6, | 10, | ____, | 21, | 28 | | 1 |

| 10 TOTAL | 10 TOTAL |

How did you do?
- Nine or ten correct? Read the **Key Facts** and then go on to topic 8: Equations and algebra.
- Eight or fewer correct? Work through this topic carefully and then retake the test!

Common number patterns

Maths is largely about seeing patterns. You need to know and be able to recognise some of the most common and useful patterns. Here are some sequences and patterns you should already know.

Multiples:	7, 14, 21, 28…	Prime numbers:	2, 3, 5, 7…
Odd numbers:	1, 3, 5, 7…	Triangular numbers:	1, 3, 6, 10…
Even numbers:	2, 4, 6, 8…	Doubling numbers:	1, 2, 4, 8…
Square numbers:	1, 4, 9, 16…	Halving numbers:	64, 32, 26, 8…
Cube numbers:	1, 8, 27, 64…		

Finding the rule

To find the missing number in a sequence, first find out the rule. It can be very helpful to write the difference between each pair of numbers along the sequence to help you find the rule.

Some sequences will go up or down by the same number each step. Others may go up or down one more or less than the previous step.

Careful: some patterns go alternately in pairs or even in threes! So, if you can't find a pattern between pairs of numbers and the numbers aren't in size order, then check to see if there are two or three sequences in one. For example, complete this sequence:

1, 2, 3, 4, 6, 6, 10, 8, 15, ____

First, write the difference between each pair of numbers:

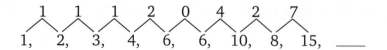

There doesn't appear to be a pattern so try looking at every other number:

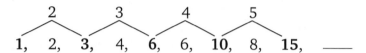

These are triangular numbers.

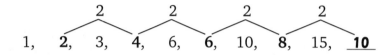

These are even numbers.

Now it's your turn!

Find the rules and then complete the sequence:

1, 2, 4, 3, 9, 5, 16, 7, _____, _____

KEY FACTS

- To find the missing number in a sequence, first find out the rule.

- Some sequences will go up or down by the same number each step. Others may go up or down one more or less than the previous step.

- Some sequences have more than one rule.

 **PARENT TIP**

Help your child to see patterns wherever possible, for example in tiles, fabrics or in flowers and plants, and relate them to number.

(8) Equations and algebra

Try this test to find out how much you already know about equations and algebra.

1 What number, when divided by 12, has an answer of 11 remainder 5? _____ ☐ 1

2 A number multiplied by itself and doubled is 242.

What is the number? _____ ☐ 1

3 Complete this table using the equation $y = 3x - 1$:

x	5		96
y	14	35	

☐ 1

4 $\frac{z}{9} = 5$ $z =$ _____ ☐ 1

5 $c - 2 = 5$ $c =$ _____ ☐ 1

6 $7 \times ? = 65 - 9$ $? =$ _____ ☐ 1

7 $35 \div 7 = 60 \div x$. Find the value of x. _____ ☐ 1

8 $\begin{array}{r} £1.95 \\ \hline 2\,|\,£\ x \end{array}$ Find the value of x. _____ ☐ 1

9 $3a + 8 = 9a - 16$. What is the value of a? _____ ☐ 1

10 If $x = 4, y = 6, z = 9$ then solve $(x + y)(y + z) =$ _____ ☐ 1

☐ 10 TOTAL ☐ 10 TOTAL

How did you do?

- Nine or ten correct? Read the **Key Facts** and then go on to topic 9: Function machines.
- Eight or fewer correct? Work through this topic carefully and then retake the test!

Equations

An **equation** is a number sentence where one thing is **equal** to something else. An equals sign, =, shows that the numbers to the left of it must be equal to, or have the same value as, the numbers to the right.

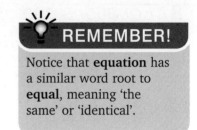

REMEMBER!

Notice that **equation** has a similar word root to **equal**, meaning 'the same' or 'identical'.

Look at this equation: $3 + 4 = 7$

Three plus four is equal to seven. Both sides of the equation are balanced. They are both equal to seven. It can be called a simple equation because it has an equals sign.

Algebra

Algebra is about finding missing (or mystery) numbers in equations. The missing numbers are often shown as letters such as a, b, c, x, y, z or symbols such as ✻, ■ or ◆.

You have to find the value of the missing number to **solve an equation**.

For example:

Solve $x = 8 - 3$.

x must be equal to the other side of the equation ($8 - 3 = 5$). So, $x = 5$.

Sometimes you might see a number next to a letter: $2y$. It is a short way of saying $2 \times y$. You might also see $\frac{10a}{5}$. It means the same as $10a \div 5$.

Now it's your turn!

Solve these equations:

$b = 2 \times 8$ $\quad b =$ ____

$25 \div 5 = y$ $\quad y =$ ____

Now look at this example:

If $x = 2$ and $y = 4$ $\quad \frac{3x}{6y} =$ ____

$$\frac{3 \times 2}{6 \times 4} = \frac{6}{24} = \frac{1}{4}$$

Now look at this example:

If $x = 10$ and $y = 5$ $\quad \frac{3x}{6y} =$ ____

$3x = 3 \times 10 = 30$

$6y = 6 \times 5 = 30$ $\quad \frac{30}{30} = 1$

Now it's your turn!

Solve these equations:

If $a = 5$ and $b = 2$ $\quad \frac{3a}{8b} =$ ____

If $x = 3$ and $y = 7$ $\quad 8x - 2y =$ ____

When the missing number is involved in a calculation on one side of the equation it can be helpful to use **inverse operations** so that the missing number is left on its own on one side of the equation. To do this, look at the sign and do the opposite to **both sides of the equation**:

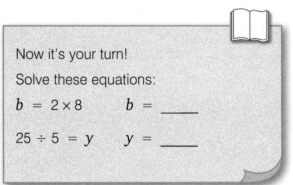

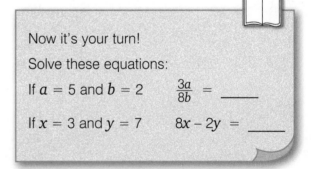

- For add, subtract. For subtract, add;
- For multiply, divide. For divide, multiply;
- For double, halve. For halve, double.

Look at these examples:

$x - 3 = 9$ What does x equal?

To leave x on its own, **add** 3 to both sides of the equation to cancel the '$- 3$':

$$x - 3 + 3 = 9 + 3$$
$$x = 9 + 3$$
$$x = 12$$

$\frac{a}{5} = 4$ What does a equal?

To leave a on its own, **multiply** both sides of the equation by 5 to cancel the '$\div 5$':

$$\frac{a}{5} \times 5 = 4 \times 5$$
$$a = 4 \times 5$$
$$a = 20$$

You may have to solve equations that need **two inverse operations** before the mystery number is left on its own on one side of the equation.

Look at this example:

$10x - 2 = 7x + 4$ What does x equal?

$$10x - 2 + 2 = 7x + 4 + 2$$
$$10x = 7x + 6$$
$$10x - 7x = 7x + 6 - 7x$$
$$3x = 6$$
$$x = 2$$

Now it's your turn!

Work out the mystery values.

$y + 7 = 18$ $y = $ _____

$\frac{z}{3} = 9$ $z = $ _____

$4a + 12 = 7a - 9$ $a = $ _____

Sometimes there are **brackets** in equations, e.g. $3 + (7 - 2)$.

To solve this, you must first do the calculation in the brackets: $7 - 2 = 5$.

The calculation then becomes $3 + 5 = 8$.

REMEMBER!

Always complete any calculations in brackets first.

- $4z = 4 \times z$
- $\dfrac{3x}{2} = 3x \div 2$
- Whatever you do to one side of an equation you must also do to the other side to keep it equal!
- If you can't work out an answer, try saying the equation out loud using the word 'something' in place of the missing number – it should make more sense:

  $\dfrac{42}{b} = 6 \longrightarrow$ "42 divided by something equals 6."

⑨ Function machines

Try this test to find out how much you already know about function machines.

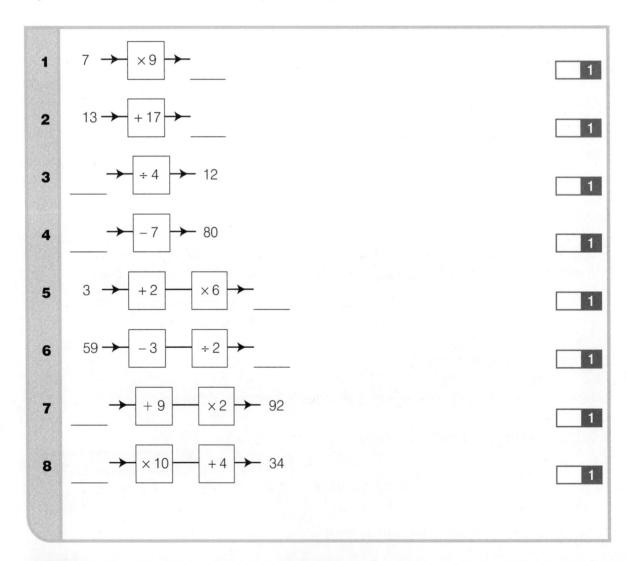

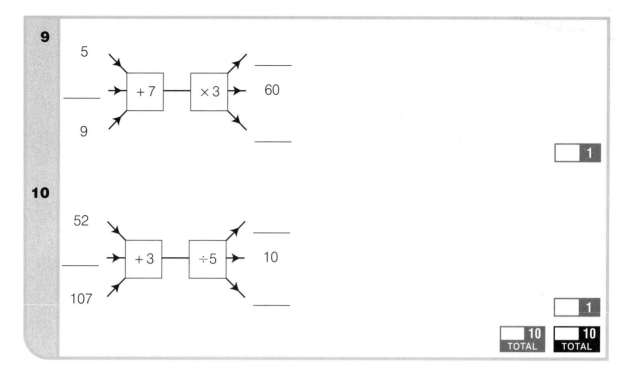

9

5

_____ → +7 — ×3 → 60

9

_____

☐ 1

10

52

_____ → +3 — ÷5 → 10

107

_____

☐ 1

☐ **10** TOTAL   ☐ **10** TOTAL

How did you do?

- Nine or ten correct? Read the **Key Facts** and then go on to topic 10: Fractions.
- Eight or fewer correct? Work through this topic carefully and then retake the test!

Introduction

Function machines are diagrams where a number is fed in from the left, one or more number operations ($+$, $\times$, $-$, $\div$) are applied to the number and then the answer comes out the right-hand side of the machine.

If the missing number is to the **right** of the function machine, apply the rule or rules that you are given, in turn, to the number on the left and find the missing number.

If the missing number is to the **left** of the function machine, apply the **inverse** of the rule or rules you are given, working backwards and find the missing number.

In this example the missing number is to the left of the function machine and you therefore need to begin with the answer to the right of the machine:

_____ → +9 — ÷4 → 7

The two number operations need to be carried out from right to left, using their inverses, so:

$\div 4$ becomes $\times 4$:

$7 \times 4 = 28$

$+ 9$ becomes $- 9$:

$28 - 9 = \mathbf{19}$

You can check your answer by working through the function machine using your answer to begin:

$$19 + 9 \div 4 = 7 \quad \checkmark$$

Now it's your turn!

Complete this function machine.

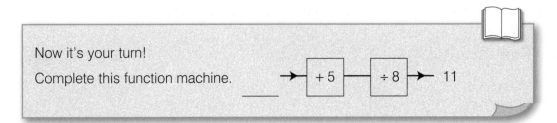

Fractions and decimals

⑩ Fractions

Try this test to find out how much you already know about fractions.

1 Find three-quarters of 180. _____ $\boxed{}\boxed{1}$

2 If $\frac{4}{5}$ of Sam's money is £5.20, how much does he have altogether?

_____ $\boxed{}\boxed{1}$

3 How many thirds is $6\frac{2}{3}$? _____ $\boxed{}\boxed{1}$

4 Arrange these fractions in order, largest first: $\frac{1}{3}$ $\frac{7}{8}$ $\frac{2}{5}$ $\frac{1}{2}$ $\frac{3}{8}$ $\frac{3}{4}$ $\frac{1}{4}$

_____ $\boxed{}\boxed{1}$

5 $7 - 3\frac{2}{7}$ = _____ $\boxed{}\boxed{1}$

6 Write the missing number: $\frac{?}{49}$ = $\frac{4}{7}$ _____ $\boxed{}\boxed{1}$

7 $\frac{3}{4} + \frac{1}{2} + \frac{3}{4}$ = _____ $\boxed{}\boxed{1}$

8 What fraction in its lowest terms is 400 m of 1 km? _____ $\boxed{}\boxed{1}$

9 Circle the two fractions that equal one whole when added together:

$\frac{4}{6}$ $\frac{5}{8}$ $\frac{1}{5}$ $\frac{1}{3}$ $\frac{3}{4}$ $\boxed{}\boxed{1}$

10 Change $\frac{43}{5}$ into a mixed number. _____ $\boxed{}\boxed{1}$

$\boxed{}\boxed{10}$ TOTAL $\boxed{}\boxed{10}$ TOTAL

How did you do?

o Nine or ten correct? Read the **Key Facts** and then go on to topic 11: Decimal fractions.

o Eight or fewer correct? Work through this topic carefully and then retake the test!

Introduction

"I find fractions confusing."

Don't worry. Fractions can be quite hard to grasp. Work through this section slowly and complete the practice activities. This will help to make things clear.

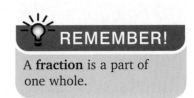

There are two parts to a simple fraction:

$$\frac{1}{2} \xleftarrow{\hspace{0.5cm}} \text{numerator}$$
$$\xleftarrow{\hspace{0.5cm}} \text{denominator}$$

The **denominator** tells you how many equal parts the whole has been divided, or cut up, into. It also gives the fraction its **name** (2 = halves, 3 = thirds, and so on).

The **numerator** tells you how many equal parts you are looking at.

Fractions like this, where the numerator and denominator are both whole numbers, are called **common** or **vulgar fractions**.

It can be useful to draw quick pictures of simple fractions.

For example:

Draw diagrams to represent $\frac{1}{8}$:

Draw a whole one. You can draw a circle or a box. Divide the shape into 8 equal pieces. Colour in one of the equal pieces.

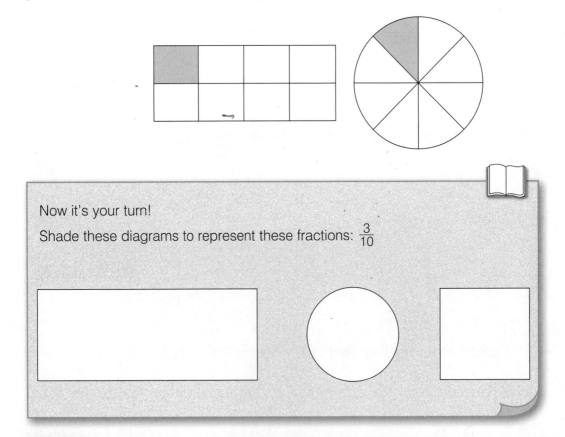

Now it's your turn!

Shade these diagrams to represent these fractions: $\frac{3}{10}$

Fractions of numbers

To find a fraction of a number, divide the number by the denominator and then multiply the answer by the numerator.

REMEMBER!

Use your times tables knowledge when working out fractions.

For example:

Find $\frac{1}{6}$ of 24.

$24 \div 6 = 4$ ⟵ divide by the denominator ⟶ $24 \div 6 = 4$

$4 \times 1 = 4$ ⟵ multiply by the numerator ⟶ $4 \times 5 = 20$

$\frac{1}{6}$ of 24 = 4

Find $\frac{5}{6}$ of 24.

$\frac{5}{6}$ of 24 = 20

Now it's your turn!

Find:

$\frac{1}{8}$ of 72 _____ $\frac{5}{9}$ of 63 _____ $\frac{2}{3}$ of 21 _____

$\frac{1}{7}$ of 49 _____ $\frac{4}{5}$ of 40 _____ $\frac{5}{12}$ of 60 _____

Mixed numbers

A mixed number is a mixture of a whole number and a fraction, like $2\frac{1}{2}$ or $7\frac{1}{4}$.

You might be asked to draw diagrams to show mixed numbers:

$1\frac{1}{3}$  $3\frac{3}{5}$

Now it's your turn!

Draw diagrams to show these mixed numbers:

$6\frac{4}{5}$ $4\frac{3}{8}$

Improper fractions

Improper fractions are top-heavy, where the numerator is **larger** than the denominator:

$\frac{13}{5}$ $\frac{7}{6}$ $\frac{97}{4}$

Improper fractions can be changed into mixed numbers using division: divide the numerator by the denominator. Work out how many times the denominator goes into the numerator. The answer becomes the whole number. The remainder becomes the numerator of the fraction. You must keep the denominator the same.

For example:

Change $\frac{13}{5}$ into a mixed number.

$$13 \div 5 = ? \text{ (How many 5s in 13?)}$$

$$13 \div 5 = 2 \text{ remainder } 3$$

$$\frac{13}{5} = 2\frac{3}{5}$$

Decimal fractions

See topic 11: Decimal fractions (p. 41).

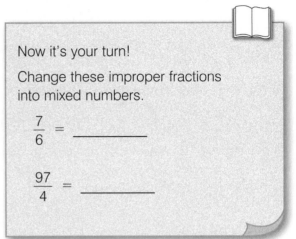

Now it's your turn!

Change these improper fractions into mixed numbers.

$$\frac{7}{6} = \underline{\hspace{3cm}}$$

$$\frac{97}{4} = \underline{\hspace{3cm}}$$

Equivalent fractions

Equivalent fractions are fractions that are **equal** to each other. For example, two quarters are exactly the same as one half:

$$\frac{2}{4} = \frac{1}{2}$$

To find a fraction equivalent to another fraction simply multiply the numerator and the denominator by the same number. (See topic 13: Ratio p. 49.)

For example, $\frac{7}{8}$ is the same as $\frac{14}{16}, \frac{21}{24}, \frac{28}{32}, \frac{35}{40}$.

Can you see why? Look at this multiplication grid which shows these equivalent fractions.

×	2	3	4	5
7	14	21	28	35
8	16	24	32	40

It can be helpful to look at the equivalence of thirds with sixths, sixths with twelfths, quarters with eighths and fifths with tenths by drawing diagrams. This diagram compares $\frac{1}{3}$s and $\frac{1}{6}$s:

Now it's your turn!

Find three equivalent fractions for each of these simple fractions:

$$\frac{4}{5} = \underline{\hspace{1.5cm}} \underline{\hspace{1.5cm}} \underline{\hspace{1.5cm}}$$

$$\frac{3}{8} = \underline{\hspace{1.5cm}} \underline{\hspace{1.5cm}} \underline{\hspace{1.5cm}}$$

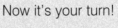

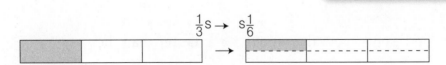

It is now easy to see that $\frac{1}{3}$ is equal to $\frac{2}{6}$.

Now it's your turn!

Draw a diagram to compare $\frac{1}{4}$s and $\frac{1}{8}$s, $\frac{1}{5}$s and $\frac{1}{10}$s and $\frac{1}{6}$s and $\frac{1}{12}$s.

Check your diagrams once you have drawn them and then ask someone else to check them.

Fraction calculations

Before you use more than one fraction in a calculation, you need to make the denominators the same. Whatever number the denominator is multiplied by, you must multiply the numerator by the same number to keep the new fraction equivalent to the fraction you started with.

Look at examples a and b:

a
$$1\frac{1}{2} + \frac{1}{4} = \underline{\hspace{1.5cm}}$$

$$1\frac{1}{2} = \frac{3}{2} \qquad \text{(Convert the mixed number to an improper fraction.)}$$

$$\frac{3 \times 2}{2 \times 2} = \frac{6}{4} \qquad \text{(Multiply by two to make both fractions quarters.)}$$

$$\frac{6}{4} + \frac{1}{4} = \frac{7}{4} = 1\frac{3}{4}$$

Don't forget that it can be helpful to draw diagrams when doing fractions. So example **a** might look like:

b $\quad 2 - \frac{3}{4} = \underline{\hspace{1.5cm}}$

$$2 = \frac{8}{4} \qquad \text{(Change 2 into quarters.)}$$

$$\frac{8}{4} - \frac{3}{4} = \frac{5}{4} = 1\frac{1}{4}$$

See how this calculation could be worked out using diagrams:

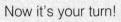

Now it's your turn!

Find the answers to these calculations.

$$\frac{1}{2} + \frac{3}{4} = \underline{\hspace{2.5cm}} \qquad\qquad \frac{3}{4} - \frac{1}{8} = \underline{\hspace{2.5cm}}$$

You could check your answers by drawing diagrams before writing.

Simplifying fractions

Fractions generally need to be expressed as simply as possible. The fraction $\frac{42}{56}$ is difficult to visualise or draw. It needs to be made as simple as possible by reducing it to its simplest or lowest terms.

To do this, find a number that will divide exactly into both the numerator and the denominator. Keep doing this until the fraction is as simple as possible.

For example:

Reduce $\frac{42}{56}$ to its simplest terms.

$$\frac{42 \div 7 = 6}{56 \div 7 = 8} \qquad \frac{6 \div 2 = 3}{8 \div 2 = 4}$$

$\frac{42}{56}$ is $\frac{3}{4}$ in its simplest terms.

Now it's your turn!

Reduce these fractions to their simplest terms:

$$\frac{5}{35} = \qquad\qquad \frac{48}{96} = \qquad\qquad \frac{70}{100} =$$

KEY FACTS

- $\dfrac{3 \longleftarrow \text{numerator}}{4 \longleftarrow \text{denominator}}$

- The numerator and denominator in a **vulgar fraction** are both whole numbers.

- To find a **fraction of a number**, divide the number by the denominator and then multiply the answer by the numerator.

- A **mixed number** is a mixture of a whole number and a fraction: $1\frac{3}{4}$

- An **improper fraction** has a larger numerator than denominator: $\frac{9}{2}$

- **Equivalent fractions** are equal to each other: $\frac{1}{3} = \frac{2}{6}$

- Before using more than one fraction in a calculation, make the denominators the same.

- To reduce a fraction to its **simplest** or **lowest terms**, divide the numerator and denominator by their highest common factor (see topic 5: Factors and multiples p. 19).

✔ PARENT TIP

The link between tables and fractions is a vital one to explain. Instead of asking "How many sixes in 36?" try asking "What is a sixth of 36?" Children who need to be able to see to understand will benefit from practical activities such as sharing out orange segments or cutting up and sharing out pizza slices.

(11) Decimal fractions

Try this test to find out how much you already know about decimal fractions.

1 Write these decimals in order, smallest first: 3.03   3.3   3.333   3.42   3.33

_____   `1`

2 By how much is 7.2 greater than 0.9?   _____   `1`

3 Write 0.84 as a common fraction in its lowest terms.   _____   `1`

4 35.791 + 5.6 =   _____   `1`

5 Circle the correct answer:

$0.2 \times 0.2 \times 0.2 =$ 0.6   8   0.8   0.0008   0.0006   0.008   `1`

6 Take 2.632 from 4.1   _____   `1`

7 Multiply 0.06 by 35   _____   `1`

8 Find the difference between 0.3 and 0.03.   _____   `1`

9 Write 600 ml as a decimal fraction of 1 litre.   _____   `1`

10 What must be added to 37.4 to equal 50?   _____   `1`

`10 TOTAL`   `10 TOTAL`

How did you do?

- Nine or ten correct? Read the **Key Facts** and then go on to topic 12: Percentages.
- Eight or fewer correct? Work through this topic carefully and then retake the test!

Introduction

"How do I work out decimal fractions?"

In a decimal fraction the digits to the left of the decimal point represent whole numbers: units, tens, hundreds, thousands, etc.

2	8	1	6	.	2	5	6
1000s	100s	10s	1s	decimal point	$\frac{1}{10}$s	$\frac{1}{100}$s	$\frac{1}{1000}$s

A decimal point separates whole numbers from numbers that are less than one.

The digits to the right of the decimal point represent parts of one whole: tenths, hundredths, thousandths, etc.

So $2816.256 = 2000 + 800 + 10 + 6 + \frac{256}{1000}$

You can remind yourself about the value of digits in different columns by looking back at topic 1: Place value p. 8.

REMEMBER!

Decimal fractions always have a decimal point.

If you divide 1 unit by 10, it becomes 0.1 $\left(\frac{1}{10}\right)$ because the digits move one place to the right. The decimal point makes 0.1 a decimal fraction.

Converting between decimal and common fractions

For 11+ Maths it is useful to know the main decimal fractions and their common fraction equivalents. These are listed below:

$\frac{1}{10} = \mathbf{0.1}$ $\frac{2}{10} = \frac{1}{5} = \mathbf{0.2}$ $\frac{3}{10} = \mathbf{0.3}$

$\frac{4}{10} = \frac{2}{5} = \mathbf{0.4}$ $\frac{5}{10} = \mathbf{0.5}$ $\frac{6}{10} = \frac{3}{5} = \mathbf{0.6}$

$\frac{7}{10} = \mathbf{0.7}$ $\frac{8}{10} = \frac{4}{5} = \mathbf{0.8}$ $\frac{9}{10} = \mathbf{0.9}$

If you need to change a common fraction to a decimal fraction that you have not learnt, it is very useful to remember that a common fraction can be thought of as a division calculation.

REMEMBER!

Estimate your answer so that the decimal point doesn't end up in the wrong place.

Look at this example:

Work out $\frac{3}{8}$ as a decimal fraction.

(We can estimate that the answer will be less than 0.5 because dividing 3 by 6 gives 0.5 and in this question 3 is divided by a number greater than 6.)

$$\begin{array}{r} 0.3 \\ 8\overline{)3.0^60000...} \end{array} \qquad \begin{array}{r} 0.3\,7 \\ 8\overline{)3.0^60^40000...} \end{array} \qquad \begin{array}{r} 0.3\,7\,5 \\ 8\overline{)3.0^60^40000...} \end{array}$$

So, $\frac{3}{8} = 0.375$.

Sometimes you will have to change decimal fractions to common fractions or mixed numbers. It is important to think carefully about tenths, hundredths and thousandths. See topic 1: Place value, p. 8, to remind yourself which column represents each of these.

The digits to the left of the decimal point (whole numbers) don't need to be changed to write a common fraction as a mixed number. Digits to the right of the decimal point must be written as the numerator in the fraction part of the mixed number.

If there is one digit to the right of the decimal point, then that digit represents the number of tenths:

$3.7 = 3\dfrac{7}{10}$

If there are two digits to the right of the decimal point, then those digits represent the number of hundredths:

$3.75 = 3\dfrac{75}{100}$

Similarly, if there are three digits to the right of the decimal point, then those digits represent the number of thousandths:

$3.758 = 3\dfrac{758}{1000}$

It is important to make sure your fraction is in its simplest terms, so $3\dfrac{75}{100}$ can be simplified to become $3\dfrac{3}{4}$. See topic 10: Fractions, p. 35, to remind yourself how to simplify fractions.

To arrange a group of decimal fractions in order, write them out one above the other, making sure the decimal points are all lined up above each other. In this example, the whole numbers are the same, so begin by looking at the tenths column:

$\downarrow$
3.241
3.124
3.412
3.214
3.421
3.142

To order from the smallest first, look for the smallest tenths digit (1) – there are two numbers with 1 tenth. It is therefore necessary to look at the hundredths column to find the smaller of the two numbers. 3.124 is the smallest.

$\downarrow$
3.124   ←

3.142   ←

Now it's your turn!

Complete the ordering of the decimal numbers used in the example above from smallest to largest.

3.124, _____, _____, _____, _____, _____

Add, subtract, multiply and divide decimal numbers

You will also need to know how to add, subtract, multiply and divide decimal numbers in 11+ Maths.

Decimals can be added and subtracted in exactly the same way as whole numbers. Keep a clear idea of what each of the numbers means by reminding yourself of the place value columns (see topic 1: Place value p. 8). It can be helpful to write the numbers you are adding or subtracting one underneath the other, always keeping the decimal point in the same column:

$$\begin{array}{r} 3.64 \\ +\ 5.29 \\ \hline 8.93 \end{array} \qquad \begin{array}{r} 7.65 \\ -\ 2.42 \\ \hline 5.23 \end{array}$$

To multiply decimal fractions, it can be useful to remember to say "of" when you see a × sign.

For example, in the calculation 0.2 × 0.2, you could ask yourself:

"What is two tenths of two tenths?" Find one tenth of 0.2 first by dividing 0.2 by 10 and then double it to find two tenths.

Or you can just ignore the decimal points to begin with, multiply $2 \times 2 = 4$ and then say: "There were two decimal places, so I have to put those back in my answer now: $0.2 \times 0.2 = 0.04$."

To divide by a decimal fraction, it can be helpful to think of the decimal fraction as a common fraction.

For example, in the calculation $5 \div 0.5$, call 0.5 a half and say:

"How many halves in 5?"

For questions where the decimal fraction isn't an obvious vulgar fraction, then saying the question out loud can still help. For example, $6 \div 1.2$ can be said as "How many 1.2s in 6?"

The question can then be solved using repeated addition:

$1.2 + 1.2 + 1.2 + 1.2 + 1.2 = 6$, therefore $6 \div 1.2 = 5$.

Now it's your turn!

Calculate the answers to these questions:

$4 \div 0.8 =$ _____ $2 \div 0.4 =$ _____ $7 \div 0.2 =$ _____

$8 \div 0.5 =$ _____ $6 \div 0.3 =$ _____ $18 \div 0.9 =$ _____

KEY FACTS

- 4.07 is an example of a decimal fraction.
- In a decimal fraction the digits to the right of the decimal point represent parts of one whole: tenths, hundredths, thousandths, and so on.
- A common (vulgar) fraction can be changed into a decimal fraction using division: $\frac{3}{8} \longrightarrow 3 \div 8 = 0.375$.
- A decimal fraction can be changed into a mixed number: $3.75 = 3\frac{75}{100} = 3\frac{3}{4}$
- Decimal fractions can be used in addition, subtraction, multiplication and division calculations.

✓ PARENT TIP

The most useful common application of decimal fractions is with pounds and pence. Encouraging your child to handle money and talk about amounts, thinking about whole pounds, tenths of pounds (10p) and hundredths of pounds (1p) will help to make decimal fractions easier to understand.

(12) Percentages

Try this test to find out how much you already know about percentages.

1   What is 10% of £4.00? _____   `1`

2   Reduce £250 by 25%. _____   `1`

3   20% of the children in a school of 420 children were absent.

How many were present? _____   `1`

4   In an after-school club there are 60 children. 60% of them are girls.

How many boys are there? _____   `1`

5   What is the new price of an item which normally costs £35,
when everything is reduced by 20% in a sale? _____   `1`

6   What is 0.45 as a percentage? _____   `1`

7   If there are 400 books in a library and 160 of them are fiction,
what percentage of them is non-fiction? _____   `1`

8   Find 21% of 4200. _____   `1`

9   The cost of a car is increased by 15% at the beginning of August.

In July the car cost £13 000.

What does it cost in August? _____   `1`

10   A filing cabinet costs £80, but you have to add on VAT at 17.5%.

What is its real price? _____   `1`

`10` TOTAL   `10` TOTAL

How did you do?

- Nine or ten correct? Read the **Key Facts** and then go on to topic 13: Ratio and proportion.
- Eight or fewer correct? Work through this topic carefully and then retake the test!

"I keep forgetting what the word 'percentage' means."

Per means '**out of**', **cent** means '**100**' (centimetre = 100 millimetres in a metre, century = 100 years).

These are the most important percentages to recognise:

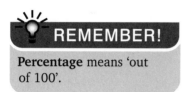

REMEMBER!

Percentage means 'out of 100'.

You know how easy it is to find $\frac{1}{10}$ or to divide by 10 (see topic 1: Place value p. 8), so 10% is a particularly useful percentage for working things out.

- $100\% = \frac{100}{100} = 1$ (one whole)
- $75\% = \frac{75}{100} = \frac{3}{4}$ (three quarters)
- $50\% = \frac{50}{100} = \frac{1}{2}$ (one half)
- $25\% = \frac{25}{100} = \frac{1}{4}$ (one quarter)
- $10\% = \frac{10}{100} = \frac{1}{10}$ (one tenth)

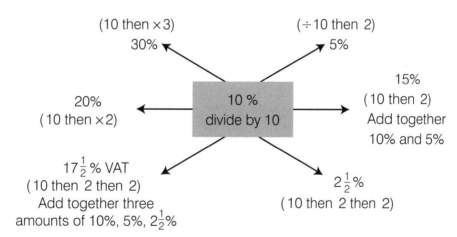

Look at this example:

Find 40% of 320.

$320 \div 10 = 32$ (Divide by 10 to find 10%.)

$32 \times 4 = 128$ (Multiply by 4 to find 40%.)

Now it's your turn!

Find 60% of 510. _____

You can also find 1% quite easily by dividing an amount by 100, but for 11+ Maths the answers can usually be worked out using 10% as a starting point.

To **increase** a given amount by a percentage, you find the given percentage and **add** it on to the original amount.

To **decrease** a given amount by a percentage, you find the given percentage and **subtract** it from the original amount.

For example:

What is the price of a £25 pair of jeans with 20% off in the sale?

$$£25.00 \div 10 = £2.50 \qquad \text{(Find 10\% of the price.)}$$

$$£2.50 \times 2 = £5.00 \qquad \text{(Double 10\% = 20\%.)}$$

$$£25.00 - £5.00 = £20 \qquad \text{(Take 20\% off the original price.)}$$

Now it's your turn!

If the price of a trampoline is £230 in January but it will cost 15% more in February, what will the trampoline cost in February?

KEY FACTS

- Percentages are all based on something being divided into 100 equal parts. 100% of something means all of it; 50% means one half of it; and 25% means one quarter of it.

- To add $17\frac{1}{2}$% VAT onto a price, divide the price by 10 to find 10%, then halve it to find 5%, halve it again to find $2\frac{1}{2}$% and then add the 10%, 5% and $2\frac{1}{2}$% amounts together to find $17\frac{1}{2}$% before adding it onto the original price.

✔ PARENT TIP

Visiting shops when there is a sale will give plenty of opportunities to help your child work out new prices by calculating and subtracting the percentage discounts.

⑬ Ratio and proportion

Try this test to find out how much you already know about ratio and proportion.

1 Nathan shares out 12 sweets. He gives Jasmin 1 sweet for every 3 sweets he takes.

How many sweets does Nathan get? _____   ☐ 1

2 Look at this pattern: ♥♥♥○○♥♥♥○○♥♥♥○○

What is the ratio of black hearts to white circles? _____   ☐ 1

3 Harley watched 45 cars go past his house. 3 in every 5 cars were silver.

How many silver cars did he see? _____   ☐ 1

4 A mother seal is fed 5 fish for every 2 fish that her baby receives.

The warden fed the mother seal 15 fish.

How many fish did her baby get? _____   ☐ 1

5 For every £5 note that Kamal puts in her money box, her dad gives her three 50p coins. Kamal's dad gave her twenty-one 50p coins.

How much had Kamal put in her money box? _____   ☐ 1

6 £6.40 is shared between Simon, Sophie, Sadie and Sanjit in the ratio 1 : 2 : 5 : 8.

How much does Sadie receive? _____   ☐ 1

7 Some Top Trump cards are won by Arif and Ethan in the ratio 5 : 4.

If Ethan has won 20, Arif will get _____.   ☐ 1

8 Susie is 12 and Angela is 8. Their aunt gives them £60 to be shared

in the ratio of their ages. How much will Angela get? _____   ☐ 1

9 In a youth group there are 91 children. There are 4 boys to every 3 girls.

How many girls are there? _____   ☐ 1

10 There are 5 milk chocolates to every 2 dark chocolates in a box of 28 sweets.

How did many dark chocolates are there in the box? _____

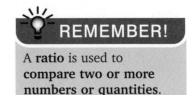

How did you do?
- Nine or ten correct? Read the **Key Facts** and then go on to topic 14: Organising and comparing information.
- Eight or fewer correct? Work through this topic carefully and then retake the test!

Ratio

A ratio is expressed as two or more numbers with a colon in between.

> **REMEMBER!**
> A **ratio** is used to compare two or more numbers or quantities.

3 : 2

This is the ratio 3 to 2 and is represented in this picture using black and white beads:

There are 3 black beads to every 2 white beads. We could also say "3 black beads for every 2 white beads".

> **REMEMBER!**
> To describe a ratio say "**to**" or "**to every**". The third and last letters of ratio spell '**to**'.

When you share something in a given ratio, you must first total the numbers in the ratio to find out how many equal parts you need to work with. This is like finding out the denominator in a fraction.

In the case of 4 : 5 : 6 the total number of equal parts would be 4 + 5 + 6 = 15. You must then find out the value of one part. To do this, divide the whole amount by the number of equal parts needed. So, for the ratio of 4 : 5 : 6 you would divide the whole amount by 15. The final step is to share out the equal parts according to the ratio.

Proportion

If the ratio of 3 black beads to every 2 white beads is used to colour 5 beads, then the proportion of black beads is 3, or **3 in every 5**, and the proportion of white beads is 2, or **2 in every 5**:

> **REMEMBER!**
> When you share out an amount using a given ratio, then each share is a **proportion** of the total amount.

Practice Test
Maths 11+

Read the instructions carefully.

- Do not begin the test or open the booklet until told to do so.

- Work as quickly and as carefully as you can.

- Each question will tell you whether to write an answer or ring the correct answer from the options given.

- You may do rough working on a separate sheet of paper.

- If you make a mistake cross out the mistake and write the new answer clearly.

- You will have 50 minutes to complete the test.

Text © Nelson Thornes Ltd

The right of Nelson Thornes Ltd to be identified as author of this work has been asserted by them in accordance with the Copyright, Designs and Patents Act 1988.

All rights reserved. No part of this publication may be reproduced or transmitted in any form or by any means, electronic or mechanical, including photocopy, recording or any information storage and retrieval system, without permission in writing from the publisher or under licence from the Copyright Licensing Agency Limited, of Saffron House, 6-10 Kirby Street, London EC1N 8TS.

Any person who commits any unauthorised act in relation to this publication may be liable to criminal prosecution and civil claims for damages.

Published in 2006 by:
Nelson Thornes Ltd
Delta Place
27 Bath Road
CHELTENHAM
GL53 7TH
United Kingdom

12 13 / 15 14 13 12

A catalogue record for this book is available from the British Library

ISBN 978 0 7487 9696 0

Page make-up by GreenGate Publishing Services, Tonbridge, Kent

Printed in China by 1010 Printing International Ltd

Published by Nelson Thornes. Nelson Thornes is not associated in any way with NFER-Nelson.

1 If you need 6 apples to make a pie, how many pies can be made with 125 apples? _____

2 In the number 58 470, the digit 4 in this number has a value of 400. What is the value of the digit 8? _____

3 A plank is 4 m 6 cm long. It is cut in half. How long is each piece? _____

This triangle has angles a, b, c and d. Angle a is 46° and angle b is 68°.

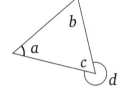

4 What is the size of angle c? _____

5 What is the size of angle d? _____

6 Jane is drawing a plan of her house. Her scale is 4 cm to 5 m. The hall is 10.5 m long. How long is the hall on her plan? _____ cm

7 Mike thought of a number. He halved it, then added 9. The answer was 45. What number did Mike think of? _____

Write the coordinates of:

8 The church (_____, _____)

9 The station (_____, _____)

10 The pet shop (_____, _____)

11 The garage (_____, _____)

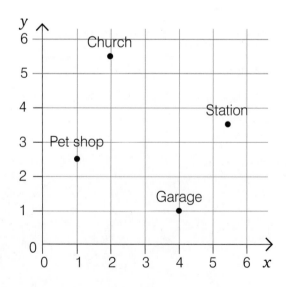

	1
	1
	1
	1
	1
	1
	1
	1
	1
	1
	1

11
TOTAL

12 Circle the group of numbers below that are all multiples of either 3 or 5.

8, 10, 12   12, 14, 15   15, 18, 20   18, 20, 22   20, 24, 26

1

13 A holiday costs £360 for an adult. It is £150 less for a child. How much is it for three adults and two children to go? _____

1

14 Circle the number with the largest value.

6.03   5.05   6.10   5.99   6.09

1

15 In the equation $6a + 7 = 55 - 2a$, what is a? _____

1

16 Here are some scores in a test: 11, 18, 9, 1, 6, 15, 3. What is the mean?
_____

1

17 Which ratio is the equivalent to 27 : 36? Circle the correct answer.

6:7   9:18   8:9   3:4

1

18 There are 45 pupils in a class. $\frac{1}{9}$ travel to school by train. $\frac{2}{5}$ travel by car. $\frac{2}{9}$ travel by bus. The rest walk to school. How many walk? _____

1

19 What percentage of this shape is shaded?
_____

1

20 420 shoppers are asked about their favourite fruit. How many like oranges?
_____

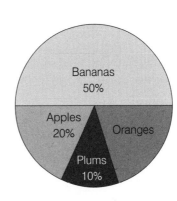

1

10
TOTAL

21 I spend 34p on the bus fare each weekday. How much do I spend a week?

_____

1

22 What is 2.467851 to two decimal places? _____

1

23 Circle the fraction with the largest value: $\frac{20}{24}$ $\frac{9}{12}$ $\frac{5}{6}$ $\frac{2}{3}$ $\frac{7}{8}$

1

24 Here are five scores in a cricket match: 11, 23, x, 44, 7. The mean score was 18. What is the value of x? _____

1

25 What does 6^5 equal? Circle the correct answer.

$5 \times 5 \times 5 \times 5 \times 5 \times 5$ $6 \times 6 \times 6 \times 6 \times 6$ 6×5 65 56

1

26 $a = \frac{3}{5}$ of b. Circle the equation below that is not correct.

$5a = 3b$ $\frac{a}{b} = \frac{3}{5}$ $3a = 5b$ $a = \frac{3}{5}b$ $b = \frac{5}{3}a$

1

The bar chart shows the number of cars that went past a traffic survey checkpoint every hour.

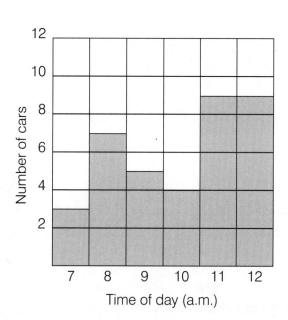

27 How many more went by at 11 a.m. than 7 a.m.? _____

1

28 How many fewer went by at 9 a.m. than 12 p.m.? _____

1

8
TOTAL

A fruit bowl contains an apple, two pears and three oranges. You choose a fruit from the bowl without looking. Say whether each pair of statements are **both** true. Circle Yes or No.

29 You have a less than even chance of picking an apple.

You have a less than even chance of picking a pear.   Yes   No

30 You have an even chance of picking an orange.

You have a greater than even chance of picking an apple.   Yes   No

31 You have a greater than even chance of picking an orange.

You have a less than even chance of picking a pear.   Yes   No

32 You have a greater than even chance of picking a pear.

You have an even chance of picking an orange.   Yes   No

33 You are certain to pick a fruit.

You have a greater than even chance of picking an orange.   Yes   No

34 The area of a rectangle is 48 cm². What could be the perimeter of the rectangle? Circle the correct answer.

12 cm   14 cm   18 cm   28 cm   30 cm

35 Jamal will be a years old in four years' time. How old was he eight years ago in terms of a? _____

36 There are 360 cars in the car park. $\frac{1}{12}$ are red. $\frac{2}{3}$ are green. The rest are silver. How many silver cars are there? _____

37 There are 300 paper clips in a box. How many paper clips in 7.5 boxes?

_____

38 Circle the number below that has the closest value to 2.

$1\frac{19}{25}$ 172.8%   1.73   172.9% $1\frac{19}{26}$

39 80 cm of a 4.4 m stretch of road need repairing. What fraction is this? Circle the correct answer.

$\dfrac{1}{9}$ $\qquad$ $\dfrac{1}{10}$ $\qquad$ $\dfrac{3}{12}$ $\qquad$ $\dfrac{4}{26}$ $\qquad$ $\dfrac{2}{11}$

40 I am half as old as my sister. In six years' time she will be 22. How old am I?

_____

Look at this room plan.

5 m

41 What is the perimeter of the room?   1 m   2 m

_____

                                                                        3 m

42 What is the area of the room?   1 m

_____

43 Carpet costs £8 a square metre. How much will it cost to carpet the room?

_____

I go to the supermarket and spend £3.50 on meat, 90p on bread, £2.50 on fruit, £3.75 on cheese, £2.15 on fruit juice and £1.45 on eggs.

44 How much have I spent? _____

45 How much change will I get from £20? _____

46 Steaks cost £4.99 each. A chef buys 125 for his restaurant. What is the total cost?

£499 $\qquad$ £625 $\qquad$ £623.75 $\qquad$ £623.25 $\qquad$ £626.25

When every space on the grid is filled in, each row and column adds up to 44.

17		**A**	44
12		15	44
	9	**B**	44
44	44	44	

47 What is the value of **A**? _____

48 What is the value of **B**? _____

1
1
1
1
1
1
1
1
1

10
TOTAL

49   How should the time 4.45 in the morning be written? Circle the correct answer.

16.45   14.45   18.45   13.45   04.45

`[  ]` 1

50   A door is 5 feet 9 inches high. Which is closest to its height in metres? Circle the correct answer.

1.5 m   1.6 m   1.7 m   1.8 m   1.9 m

`[  ]` 1

`[  ]` 2
TOTAL

Look at this example:

£4.80 is shared between Adam, Aisha and Bethany in the ratio 3 : 1 : 2. What proportion of the money does Bethany receive?

$3 + 1 + 2 = 6$ (Find the total number of equal parts.)

£4.80 ÷ 6 = £0.80   (Divide the amount to be shared by the number of equal parts.)

£0.80 × 2 = £1.60   (In the given ratio, Bethany is given 2 of the equal parts.)

Bethany receives £1.60.

Now it's your turn!

48 Top Trump cards are shared between Lucy, Salim, Hannah and Declan in the ratio 1 : 2 : 4 : 1. What proportion of the cards does Salim receive?

_____

KEY FACTS

- A **ratio** is used to **compare two numbers or quantities**.

- Ratio is said as "**to** every" or "for every" and is often written using a colon between two numbers (2 : 1). This is the ratio "2 to 1".

- When you share out an amount using a given ratio, then each share is a **proportion** of the total amount.

- Proportion can be said as "**in** every".

 PARENT TIP

Try using props such as orange segments, coins, sweets, etc. to help work out ratio and proportion questions. This can help your child to visualise the amounts involved.

 PARENT TIP

For more ratio practice, explain that the scale given on a map is a ratio. A scale of 1 : 100 000 means 1 centimetre (cm) on the map represents 100 000 cm (= 1000 m = 1 km) in real life. Work out together some actual distances of towns or places of interest from where you live.

Handling data

⑭ Organising and comparing information

Try this test to find out how much you already know about organising and comparing information.

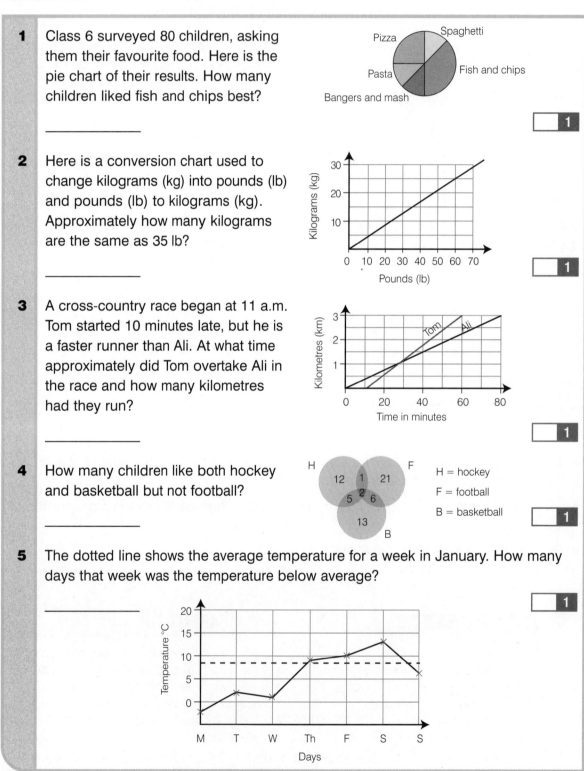

1 Class 6 surveyed 80 children, asking them their favourite food. Here is the pie chart of their results. How many children liked fish and chips best?

Pizza Spaghetti
Pasta Fish and chips
Bangers and mash

_____ `1`

2 Here is a conversion chart used to change kilograms (kg) into pounds (lb) and pounds (lb) to kilograms (kg). Approximately how many kilograms are the same as 35 lb?

_____ `1`

3 A cross-country race began at 11 a.m. Tom started 10 minutes late, but he is a faster runner than Ali. At what time approximately did Tom overtake Ali in the race and how many kilometres had they run?

_____ `1`

4 How many children like both hockey and basketball but not football?

H = hockey
F = football
B = basketball

_____ `1`

5 The dotted line shows the average temperature for a week in January. How many days that week was the temperature below average?

_____ `1`

6 Maryam went cycling and timed herself. Later, she made this graph. What was her speed in km/h (kilometres per hour)?

_____

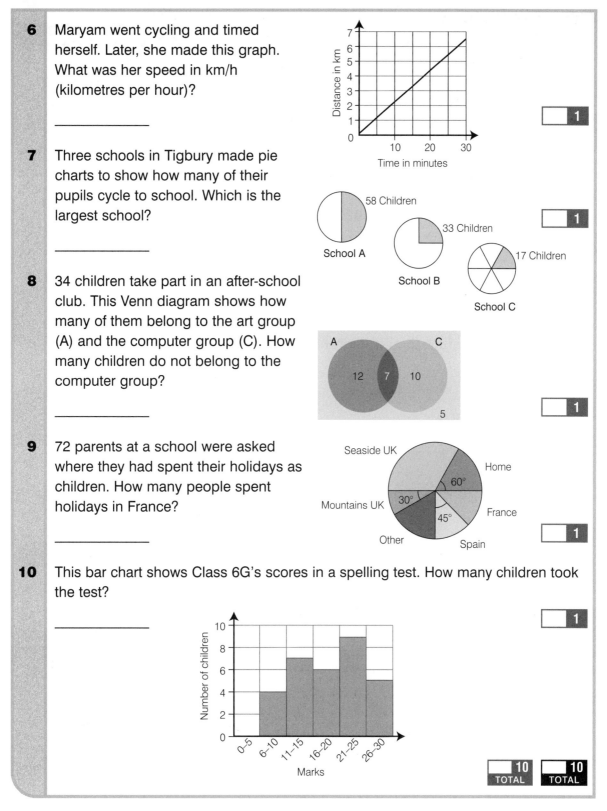

7 Three schools in Tigbury made pie charts to show how many of their pupils cycle to school. Which is the largest school?

_____

8 34 children take part in an after-school club. This Venn diagram shows how many of them belong to the art group (A) and the computer group (C). How many children do not belong to the computer group?

_____

9 72 parents at a school were asked where they had spent their holidays as children. How many people spent holidays in France?

_____

10 This bar chart shows Class 6G's scores in a spelling test. How many children took the test?

_____

1

1

1

1

1

10 TOTAL

10 TOTAL

How did you do?

- Nine or ten correct? Read the **Key Facts** and then go on to topic 15: Mean, median, mode and range.
- Eight or fewer correct? Work through this topic carefully and then retake the test!

Data

Data can be numbers or words and is usually collected by observing, questioning or measuring. In 11+ Maths you need to be able to understand different ways of showing data, such as line graphs, block graphs, pie charts, tables of information and Venn diagrams.

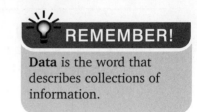

You also need to be able to answer questions about data shown in these ways. If you have to draw graphs or charts yourself, you must be very careful to choose a sensible way of showing the numbers from your data. Organising your information into tables may show patterns or similarities in your data.

Graphs

Graphs can have bars, lines or pictures representing the data.

Every graph has two lines, called axes, the plural of axis (*x*-axis and *y*-axis), which join or intersect like this:

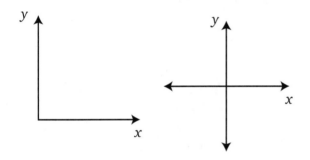

x and *y* are mystery amounts in maths and you must label the axes to make it clear what they represent.

The *x*-axis is always **horizontal** (straight across, like the horizon).

The *y*-axis is always **vertical** (straight up or down).

Pie charts

A pie chart is a circle divided into sections to show how something is shared or divided into groups. Look at this pie chart; it shows how much time children in Year 6 spend doing different activities between 4 p.m. and 8 p.m.

From these results, we can see, for example, that they spend $\frac{1}{8}$ of their time doing homework, $\frac{1}{4}$ of their time playing and $\frac{1}{12}$ of their time going to clubs.

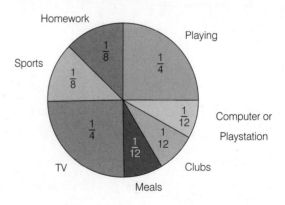

The following facts can help you answer many questions about pie charts.

$360°$	$= 100\%$	$= 1$
$180°$	$= 50\%$	$= \frac{1}{2}$
$90°$	$= 25\%$	$= \frac{1}{4}$

REMEMBER!

There are 360° in a circle, 180° in a semicircle and 90° in a right angle.

Look again at the pie chart on page 54. What percentage of their time do the children spend watching TV and doing sports? TV _____ Sports _____ .

Venn diagrams

Each circle is labelled to show which items of data can be included in it and which cannot. Where two or more circles overlap, the data that can be included in both or all circles is written in the overlapped section.

REMEMBER!

Venn diagrams are diagrams in which the data is organised into circles.

1 Look at the table below; it shows the type of pets that 25 children in Year 6 have.

Dogs	6
Cats	12
Rabbits	2
Mice	1
Fish	1
Hamsters	4
No pets	6

2 These results can be displayed in a Venn diagram such as the one shown here.

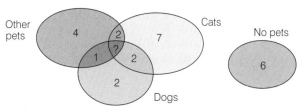

How many children have a dog, a cat and another pet? _____

1 On squared paper, draw a bar chart to show the number of sandwiches sold at lunchtimes in a café last week.

    Mon. 20   Tues. 10   Wed. 5   Thurs. 15   Fri. 20   Sat. 30

2 Draw a pie chart to show the same results in a different way.

KEY FACTS

- **Data** describes collections of information.
- **Graphs** have an *x*-**axis** (horizontal) and a *y*-**axis** (vertical).
- **Pie charts** are circles split up into sections to represent different groups of data.
- **Venn diagrams** also use circles to organise data, but only data meeting the given rule for a circle can be included in it.

(15) Mean, median, mode and range

Try this test to find out how much you already know about the mean, median, mode and range.

1 Find the mean of 5, 6, 7, 8 and 9. _____ [1]

2 Mr Singh travelled these distances in five days.

Day	Mon.	Tues.	Wed.	Thurs.	Fri.
Distance travelled	155 km	95 km	150 km	115 km	105 km

What was his average daily journey? _____ [1]

3 A car travelled 243 km in three hours. What was the average speed in km/h (kilometres per hour)? _____ [1]

4 What is the mode for these Year 6 test results? _____ [1]

20	20	13	14	19	19	19	16	17	19	19	10	18	13	19	19	16	19	20	19	15

5 For the same set of results above, find the range. _____ [1]

6 Which number in this set of numbers is the median?

16, 12, 35, 13, 15, 24, 4 _____ [1]

7 What is the average or mean of these numbers? 37, 23, 71, 90, 24 _____ [1]

8 The average of three numbers is 12. What is the total of the three numbers?

_____ [1]

9 Dan is 10 years 5 months, Pip is 11 years 6 months and Farouk is 10 years 10 months. What is the mean age of the three children?

_____ [1]

10 A motorist travelled to York in $2\frac{1}{2}$ hours at an average speed of 64 km/h.

What distance did she travel? _____ [1]

[ ] 10 TOTAL [ ] 10 TOTAL

How did you do?
- Nine or ten correct? Read the **Key Facts** and then go on to topic 16: Probability.
- Eight or fewer correct? Work through this topic carefully and then retake the test!

Range

The range of a set of numbers is the difference between the smallest number and the largest number.

Mode, median and mean

There are three different types of average of a set of data: the **mode**, the **median** and the **mean**.

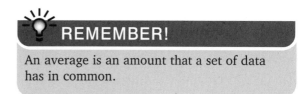

REMEMBER!

An average is an amount that a set of data has in common.

The **mode** is the number in the data that comes up most often.

The **median** is the middle number when they are put in order of size. If there are two middle numbers, you have to add those two numbers together and halve them to find the median.

The **mean** is found by adding together all the numbers in the set of data and dividing by how many numbers there are in the set.

You can find the **average** of a set of numbers in exactly the same way as the mean.

Look at this example:

Find the range, mode, median and mean for this set of times table test results:

| 7 | 10 | 7 | 5 | 9 | 9 | 10 | 6 | 9 |

Range: 10 − 5 = **5**

Mode: **9** (9 appears more times than any other score)

Median: **9**

| 5 | 6 | 7 | 7 | **9** | 9 | 9 | 10 | 10 |

Mean: 5 + 6 + 7 + 7 + 9 + 9 + 9 + 10 + 10 = 72   72 ÷ 9 = **8**

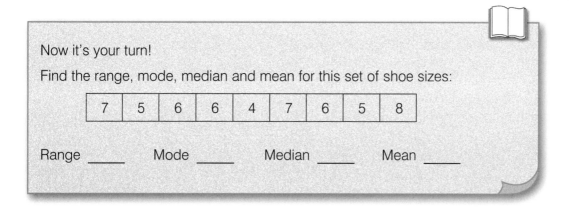

Now it's your turn!

Find the range, mode, median and mean for this set of shoe sizes:

| 7 | 5 | 6 | 6 | 4 | 7 | 6 | 5 | 8 |

Range _____   Mode _____   Median _____   Mean _____

- **Range** – the difference between largest and smallest.
- **Mode** – the number that appears the most often.
- **Median** – the number in the middle when put in size order.
- **Mean** – the average of a set of numbers.

(16) Probability

Try this test to find out how much you already know about probability.

In a bag are six balls numbered 1 to 6. What is the probability that you would take out:

1 the ball numbered 5? _____ [1]

2 a ball which has an even number on it? _____ [1]

3 What is the probability that you will pick a king of hearts from a pack of 52 cards?

_____ [1]

4 A boy throws two fair dice once each. Circle the probability that he gets a double 6:

$\frac{1}{6}$ $\quad$ $\frac{1}{12}$ $\quad$ $\frac{1}{24}$ $\quad$ $\frac{1}{36}$ $\quad$ $\frac{1}{66}$ $\quad$ $\frac{2}{12}$ $\quad$ $\frac{6}{6}$ [1]

5 If he throws only one fair die, circle the probability of getting a 3:

$\frac{1}{3}$ $\quad$ $\frac{1}{4}$ $\quad$ $\frac{1}{5}$ $\quad$ $\frac{1}{6}$ [1]

6 What is the probability that he gets a 3 or a 4 with one fair die? _____ [1]

7 If a coin is thrown 10 times, how many times is it likely to land on heads?

_____ [1]

In a bag there are 3 red balls and 4 blue balls.

8 Circle the probability of picking a red ball: $\quad$ $\frac{3}{8}$ $\quad$ $\frac{3}{7}$ $\quad$ $\frac{3}{6}$ $\quad$ $\frac{3}{5}$ $\quad$ $\frac{3}{4}$ [1]

9 Circle the probability of picking a blue ball: $\quad$ 0 $\quad$ $\frac{1}{2}$ $\quad$ $\frac{4}{7}$ $\quad$ $\frac{3}{7}$ $\quad$ $\frac{3}{4}$ [1]

10 Circle the probability of picking a yellow ball: $\quad$ 0 $\quad$ $\frac{1}{2}$ $\quad$ $\frac{4}{7}$ $\quad$ $\frac{3}{7}$ $\quad$ $\frac{3}{4}$ [1]

10 TOTAL $\quad$ 10 TOTAL

How did you do?

- Nine or ten correct? Read the **Key Facts** and then go on to topic 17: 2D shapes: circles, angles and bearings.
- Eight or fewer correct? Work through this topic carefully and then retake the test!

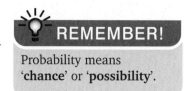

REMEMBER!

Probability means 'chance' or 'possibility'.

Introduction

The **probability** of something happening is the likelihood or chance of it happening. What is the likelihood of something happening? What chance do you have?

If something is certain to happen, its probability is 1. If something is certain not to happen, its probability is 0.

If an event is neither certain, nor certain not to happen, then its probability is expressed as a fraction. Take, for example, tossing a coin and it landing heads up. There is a 1 in 2 chance of this happening, so its probability is:

The number of the possibilities in which you are interested. (Heads only, 1 possibility.)

The number of possibilities $\longrightarrow \dfrac{1}{2} \longleftarrow$ (Heads or tails, 2 possibilities.)
(Heads only, 1 possibility).

Sometimes, as with throwing two dice, there may be many different combinations that are possible. Each die (or dice) has six numbers, so throwing two dice you have 6×6 possibilities: 36 in all. So to get the number 2 on both dice, it is a chance of 1 in 36 or $\dfrac{1}{36}$.

Look at this example:

If you roll two dice, what is the probability that the total of the two dice is 6?

Options:

Dice 1	Dice 2
1	5
5	1
2	4
4	2
3	3

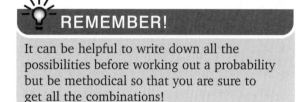

REMEMBER!

It can be helpful to write down all the possibilities before working out a probability but be methodical so that you are sure to get all the combinations!

The total 6 can be made in 5 different ways. There are 36 possibilities in total, so the probability of the total being 6 is $\dfrac{5}{36}$.

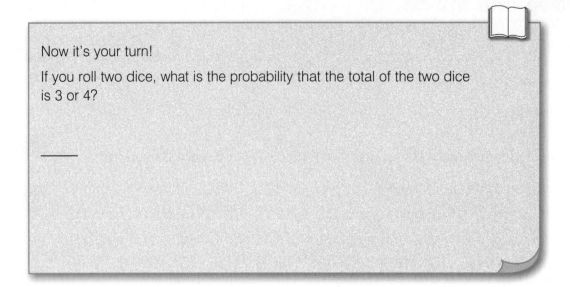

Now it's your turn!

If you roll two dice, what is the probability that the total of the two dice is 3 or 4?

In 11+ Maths, you may have to find out about the probability of picking balls or numbers out of a bag, throwing a die or dice, tossing coins or choosing playing cards from a pack. With dice or coins, it is possible to have weighted or unfair ones, so very often a question will tell you that the dice or coins are fair. Then there is no possibility of cheating!

KEY FACTS

- The **probability** of something happening is the likelihood or chance of it happening.
- A probability of 1 means an event is certain to happen.
- A probability of 0 means an event is certain not to happen.
- All other probabilities are given as a fraction between 0 and 1.

✔ PARENT TIP

It can be helpful to have props to hand when working through questions where the probability is uncertain, for example a bag of marbles, a few coins, a pack of playing cards, dice, pencils, etc.

Shape and space

⑰ 2D shapes: circles, angles and bearings

Try this test to find out how much you already know about circles, angles and bearings.

1 What is the smaller angle between 4 and 8 on a clock face? _____ [ ] 1

2 From 360°, subtract the sum of two right angles. _____ [ ] 1

3 Give the size of each angle at the centre of this regular hexagon.

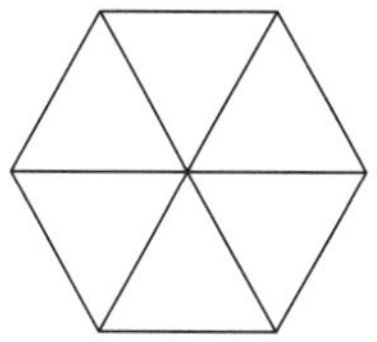

_____ [ ] 1

4 What is the size of angle x? _____ [ ] 1

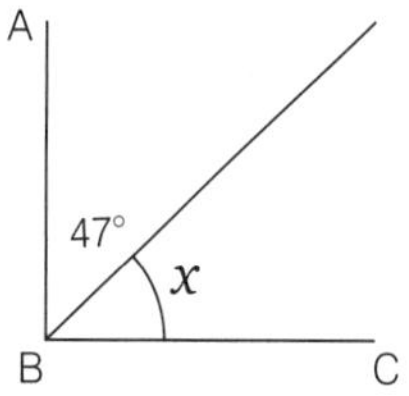

A

47°

x

B   C

5 The radius of this circle is 1.9 cm.

Find the length of AB in millimetres (mm).

_____

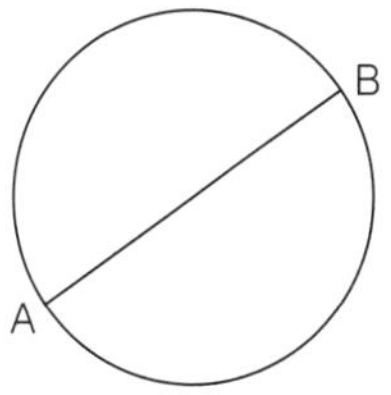

B

A

[ ] 1

6 How many degrees in the angle marked z?

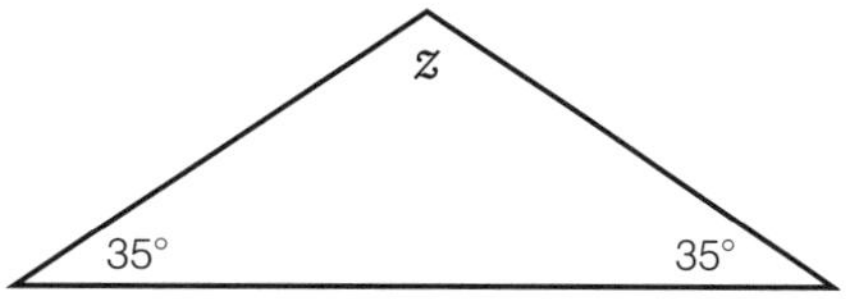

_____ [ ] 1

z

35°   35°

7 Find the radius of the largest circle that can be drawn in this square. _____ [ ] 1

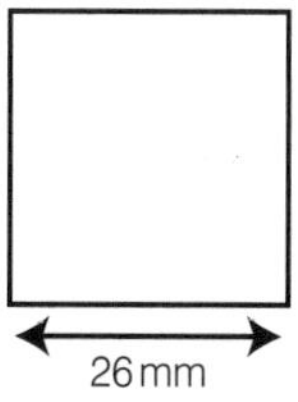

26 mm

8   Which line is perpendicular to AB?

_____

9   If you are facing SE and you turn 135°
        anticlockwise, in which direction are
        you now facing?

_____

10 These two circles are concentric.
        The inner circle has a diameter of 15 mm.
        The outer circle has a diameter of 25 mm.
        Find the width of the shaded ring in mm.

_____

	1

	1

	1

	10			10
	TOTAL			TOTAL

How did you do?
- Nine or ten correct? Read the **Key Facts** and then go on to topic 18: 2D shapes: triangles.
- Eight or fewer correct? Work through this topic carefully and then retake the test!

Circles

You need to know the names of certain parts of a circle:

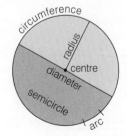

REMEMBER!

If you draw a circle using a pair of compasses, the hole left by the sharp point is the centre, or the middle, of the circle.

Concentric circles share the same centre point but the radius of each circle is different.

It is important to know the relationship between the diameter and radius of a circle:

$D = 2r$, which is shorthand for **the diameter is two times the radius**.

Therefore, $r = \frac{1}{2}d$ which means **the radius is half the diameter**.

A circle has an infinite number of radii (or radiuses) and an infinite number of diameters, which means that you can draw a radius or a diameter anywhere on a circle as long as it includes the centre.

Angles

An **angle** tells us how far something turns or rotates.

Angles are measured in **degrees**. There are 360 degrees (360°) in a circle. This makes a full turn.

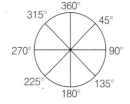

When a circle is divided into quarters, four **right angles** (90°) are made. This is the same as a quarter turn.

It is very important that you recognise a **right angle**. It looks like the corner of a square or a piece of paper.

Two lines are **perpendicular** if they are at right angles to each other. One line is perpendicular to the other.

Line AC is at right angles to line BC   Line AC is perpendicular to line BD

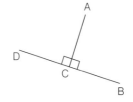

Two lines are **parallel** if they travel in the same direction and are the same distance apart all along their lengths.

Parallel lines never meet and therefore will never make an angle between them.

Parallel lines do not have to be straight. Think of railway tracks!

An angle of 180° is a straight line. It can be thought of as two right angles (90°) together. Your protractor will probably have 180° as its largest amount. It is half a complete turn or a semicircle.

Angles less than 90° are called **acute**. Acute means **sharp**.

Angles greater than 90° but less than 180° are called **obtuse**. Obtuse means **blunt**.

Angles greater than 180° are called **reflex**.

Every right angle or acute angle has a matching or complementary reflex angle. The two angles add up to make 360°, a complete turn.

Bearings

A **bearing** is the angle between the direction north and the direction in which something is travelling. As well as north there are other directions, which are marked on a compass:

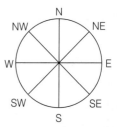

See how the compass points match the degrees shown on the circle. These are the bearing measurements.

KEY FACTS

- There are 360° in a circle.
- An **acute angle** is less than 90°.
- A **right angle** is 90°.
- An **obtuse angle** is between 90° and 180°.
- A **reflex angle** is greater than 180°.
- **Perpendicular lines** are at right angles to each other.
- **Parallel lines** never meet but run the same distance apart from each other for their entire length.
- A **compass** is used to find a **bearing**: the angle between north and the direction in which something is travelling.
- The points on a compass are N, NE, E, SE, S, SW, W and NW.

✔ PARENT TIP

There are many maths terms in this topic. Find ways of making these real. Find examples of right angles (e.g. cupboard corners), parallel/ perpendicular lines (e.g. table edges or door frames), or set out on a treasure hunt with clues that need a compass to find bearings.

---

⑱ 2D shapes: triangles

Try this test to find out how much you already know about triangles.

1 Two angles of a triangle measure 80° and 45°. Find the third angle.

_____ [1]

2 What is the name of this triangle?

_____

60° 60°

[1]

3 What is the area of this triangle in cm²?

_____

7 cm

12 cm

[1]

4 In this right-angled triangle, what is the size in degrees of the angle marked a?

a

160°

_____ [1]

5 What is the name of a triangle with sides of three different lengths and angles of three different sizes?

_____ [1]

6 What is the size in degrees of angle x? _____ [1]

x

55°

55°

7 Draw a circle around the acute-angled triangle. [1]

A B C D E

8 What is the area of this triangle in cm²? [1]

_____

☐ 1 cm²

9 How many lines of symmetry does an isosceles triangle have? [1]

_____

10 Draw a circle around the name of a triangle that is more frequently called an equilateral triangle. [1]

right-angled triangle   acute-angled triangle   obtuse-angled triangle

10 TOTAL   10 TOTAL

How did you do?
- Nine or ten correct? Read the **Key Facts** and then go on to topic 19: 2D shapes: quadrilaterals and polygons.
- Eight or fewer correct? Work through this topic carefully and then retake the test!

Types of triangle

"Triangles all look very similar to me."

Triangles can be named according to their sides and sorted into different groups:

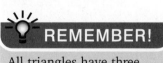

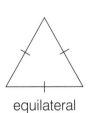
equilateral

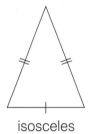
isosceles

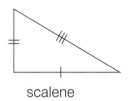
scalene

An **equilateral** triangle has **three equal sides** and three equal angles.

An **isosceles** triangle has **two equal sides** and two equal angles.

A **scalene** triangle has **no equal sides** and no equal angles.

Triangles can also be named according to their angles:

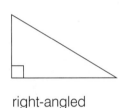
right-angled

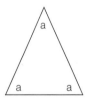
acute-angled

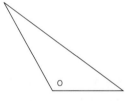
obtuse-angled

A **right-angled** triangle has **one right angle**.

An **acute-angled** triangle has **three acute angles**.

An **obtuse-angled** triangle has **one obtuse angle**.

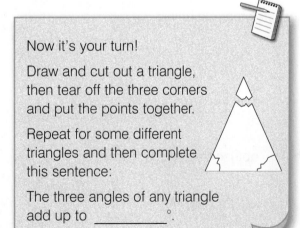

Now it's your turn!

Draw and cut out a triangle, then tear off the three corners and put the points together.

Repeat for some different triangles and then complete this sentence:

The three angles of any triangle add up to _____°.

PARENT TIP

Spotting and naming triangles (e.g. road or warning signs) while out and about can be fun and useful. This is a good game to play in the car.

Area of a triangle

To find the area of any triangle: imagine it in a rectangle, find the area of the rectangle and then halve that amount.

$$A = \tfrac{1}{2}(b \times h)$$

The area of a triangle (A) is its base (b) multiplied by its height (h), all divided by 2.

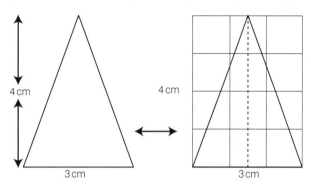

The area of this triangle is:

$$\tfrac{1}{2}(3\text{ cm} \times 4\text{ cm}) = 6\text{ cm}^2$$

See topic 20: Perimeter and area (p. 72) for a description of the units of measurement used to represent area.

Now it's your turn!

Calculate the area of these triangles:

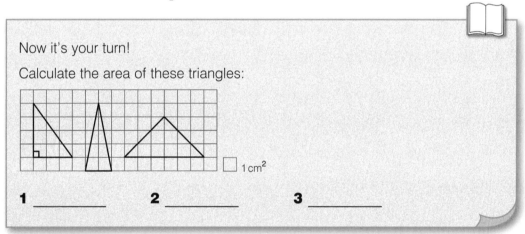

$\square$ 1 cm²

1 _____   **2** _____   **3** _____

KEY FACTS

- **Equilateral** triangle – three equal sides and angles.
- **Isosceles** triangle – two equal sides and angles.
- **Scalene** triangle – no equal sides or angles.
- **Right-angled** triangle – one right angle.
- **Acute-angled** triangle – three acute angles.
- **Obtuse-angled** triangle – one obtuse angle.
- Area of a triangle = $\tfrac{1}{2}$(base × height).

⑲ 2D shapes: quadrilaterals and polygons

Try this test to find out how much you already know about quadrilaterals and polygons.

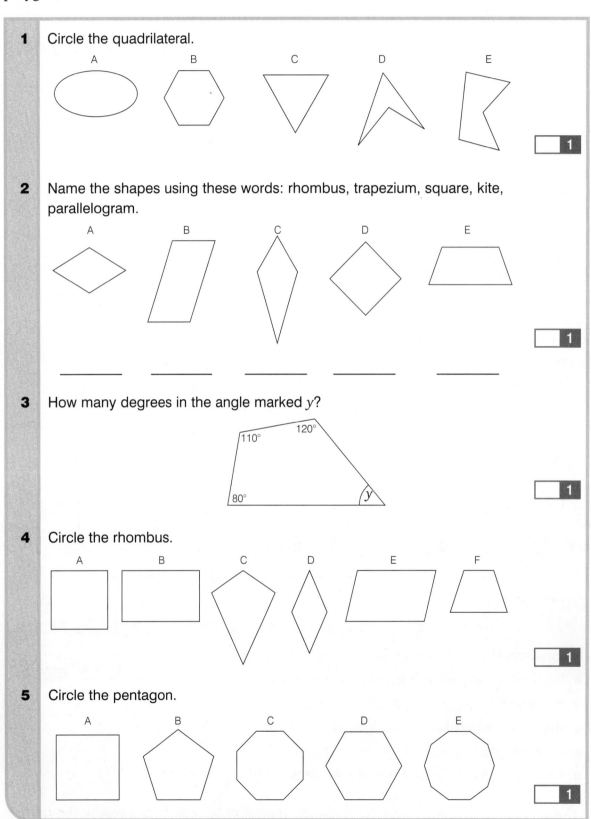

1 Circle the quadrilateral.

| A | B | C | D | E |

1

2 Name the shapes using these words: rhombus, trapezium, square, kite, parallelogram.

| A | B | C | D | E |

1

_____   _____   _____   _____   _____

3 How many degrees in the angle marked *y*?

110°   120°
80°   *y*

1

4 Circle the rhombus.

| A | B | C | D | E | F |

1

5 Circle the pentagon.

| A | B | C | D | E |

1

6 Draw the lines of symmetry on this rectangle.

[ ] 1

7 Draw the lines of symmetry on this heptagon.

[ ] 1

8 Find in degrees the size of one of the angles marked z. _____   [ ] 1

9 A 20p coin is based on which polygon? _____   [ ] 1

10 What two shapes are used to make this tile pattern?

_____ and _____   [ ] 1

[ ] 10 TOTAL   [ ] 10 TOTAL

How did you do?
- Nine or ten correct? Read the **Key Facts** and then go on to topic 20: Perimeter and area.
- Eight or fewer correct? Work through this topic carefully and then retake the test!

Quadrilaterals

Quadrilaterals have four sides and also have four angles. If you join up the opposite angles of a quadrilateral, you form its **diagonals**.

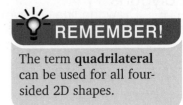

REMEMBER!

The term **quadrilateral** can be used for all four-sided 2D shapes.

You need to know the names and properties of these quadrilaterals:

- A **square** has four equal sides, four right angles and four lines of symmetry.

  A

- A **rhombus** also has four equal sides, but two equal acute angles, two equal obtuse angles and two lines of symmetry.

  B

- A **rectangle** has two pairs of parallel sides of equal length, four right angles and two lines of symmetry. Rectangles are sometimes called **oblongs**.

  C

- A **parallelogram** has two pairs of parallel sides, two equal acute angles and two equal obtuse angles. It has no lines of symmetry.

  D

- A **kite** has two pairs of sides that are adjacent, or next to each other. It has one pair of opposite equal angles and one line of symmetry.

  E

- A **trapezium** looks like a triangle with its head chopped off! Two of its sides are parallel.

  F

"The names of some of these four-sided shapes are hard to remember."

This is where a mnemonic may help. Try making up a rhyme or silly story to learn the names and practise drawing and labelling the six quadrilaterals until you know them.

Now it's your turn!

Draw and cut out a quadrilateral, then tear off the four corners and put the points together.

Repeat for some different quadrilaterals and then complete this sentence:

The four angles of any quadrilateral add up to _____ °.

Polygons

The sides of a **regular polygon** are the same length and all angles are equal. An **irregular polygon** has sides and angles that are not the same.

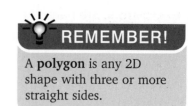

REMEMBER!

A **polygon** is any 2D shape with three or more straight sides.

You need to know the names of these regular polygons and recognise them:

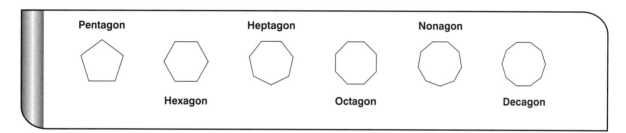

Pentagon   Heptagon   Nonagon

Hexagon   Octagon   Decagon

A **pentagon** has **five** sides.

A **hexagon** has **six** sides. The cross section of some pencils is hexagonal.

A **heptagon** has **seven** sides. A 50p coin is a heptagon.

REMEMBER!

The more sides a polygon has, the more it resembles a circle.

An **octagon** has **eight** sides, just as an **oct**opus has eight tentacles and an **oct**ave is eight notes on a scale.

A **nonagon** has **nine** sides.

A **decagon** has **ten** sides.

Now it's your turn!

1 Draw a 2D arrow shape in your notebook.

2 Can you name it according to its properties?

3 Does it have any lines of symmetry? If so, draw them.

4 Draw all lines of symmetry on a regular polygon. Where do they meet?

KEY FACTS

- **Quadrilaterals** are four-sided 2D shapes.
- **Polygons** are 2D shapes with three or more straight sides.
- The sides of a **regular polygon** are the same length and all angles are equal. All other polygons are irregular.

- Polygons are named according to the number of sides:

Name of polygon	Number of sides
pentagon	5
hexagon	6
heptagon	7
octagon	8
nonagon	9
decagon	10

⑳ Perimeter and area

Try this test to find out how much you already know about perimeter and area.

1 The perimeter of a garden is 72 m. Its length is twice its width.

Find its width in metres. _____

⬚ 1

2 An ornamental pond looks like this:

What is the perimeter of the pond in metres? _____

⬚ 1

3 How many tiles each measuring 20 cm × 20 cm would be needed to cover a work surface with measurements of 1 m × 60 cm?

_____

⬚ 1

4 Find the area of a square whose perimeter is 16 cm. _____

⬚ 1

5 Find the area of side C. _____

⬚ 1

6 Find the area of a barn which is 11 m long and 6 m wide.

_____

[1]

7 What is the approximate area of this island in square metres? _____

[1]

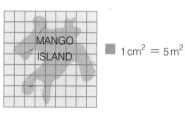

8 The perimeter of a regular hexagon is 8.4 cm.

Find the length of one side in millimetres. _____

[1]

9 What is the area of the cross-shaped paths in this garden?

Give the unit of measurement in your answer. _____

[1]

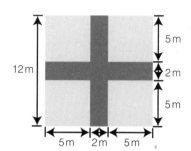

10 Which two rectangles have the same area?

_____ and _____

[1]

	A	B	C	D
Length	8 cm	4 cm	7 cm	8 cm
Width	$2\frac{1}{2}$ cm	3 cm	3 cm	$1\frac{1}{2}$ cm

10		10
TOTAL		TOTAL

How did you do?

○ Nine or ten correct? Read the **Key Facts** and then go on to topic 21: 3D shapes.

○ Eight or fewer correct? Work through this topic carefully and then retake the test!

Perimeter

The **perimeter** of a 2D shape is the total distance round the edge of the shape.

To find the perimeter of this rectangle, add all the measurements of the sides together.

$5 \text{ cm} + 3 \text{ cm} + 5 \text{ cm} + 3 \text{ cm} = 16 \text{ cm}$

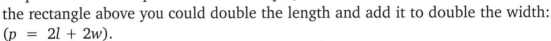

The perimeter of this shape is 16 cm.

A quick way to work out the perimeter of a shape is to use multiplication. For example, for the rectangle above you could double the length and add it to double the width: $(p = 2l + 2w)$.

$$l = 2 \times 5 = 10 \text{ cm}$$
$$w = 2 \times 3 = 6 \text{ cm}$$
$$p = 16 \text{ cm}$$

To find the perimeter of an irregular shape, find a starting point and add up the lengths of all sides until you get back to the starting point.

Area

The **area** of a 2D shape is the space inside the perimeter, which could be coloured in.

To find the area of this rectangle, multiply its length by its width.

$5 \text{ cm} \times 3 \text{ cm} = 15 \text{ cm}^2$

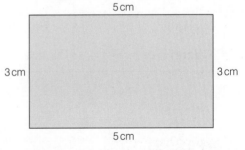

The area of this shape is 15 cm².

To find the area of an irregular shape, you may have to count squares or split it up into squares or rectangles. Then count the whole squares within the shape followed by those squares where half or more than half of the square is included in the shape. The total is an approximate estimate of the shape's area.

Think of a **perimeter hedge** going round the **edge** of a really muddy field!

Look at this example:

What are the width and area of a rectangular field if the perimeter is 260 m and the length of the field is 90 m?

90 m

90 m

$260 \text{ m} - 90 \text{ m} - 90 \text{ m} = 80 \text{ m}$

Width: $80 \text{ m} \div 2 = \textbf{40 m}$

Area: $90 \text{ m} \times 40 \text{ m} = \textbf{3600 m}^2$ (length × width)

Now it's your turn!

If the area of a rectangle is 91 cm^2 and the width is 7 cm, what is:

the length? _____   the perimeter? _____

KEY FACTS

- The **perimeter** of a 2D shape is the total distance round the **edge** of the shape and can be measured in mm, cm, m or km.

- The **area** of a 2D shape is the space **inside** the perimeter, which could be coloured in. It can be measured in cm^2, m^2 or km^2.

- To calculate the perimeter or area of a shape you need to know the distance along each side of the shape.

PARENT TIP

Any opportunities for practical measuring in centimetres or metres are beneficial here. For example, set tasks such as calculating the area and/or perimeter of: a piece of A4 paper, an exercise book or some postcards using a ruler; or a rectangular table, a TV screen, a single bed or a door using a tape measure.

21 3D shapes

Try this test to find out how much you already know about 3D shapes.

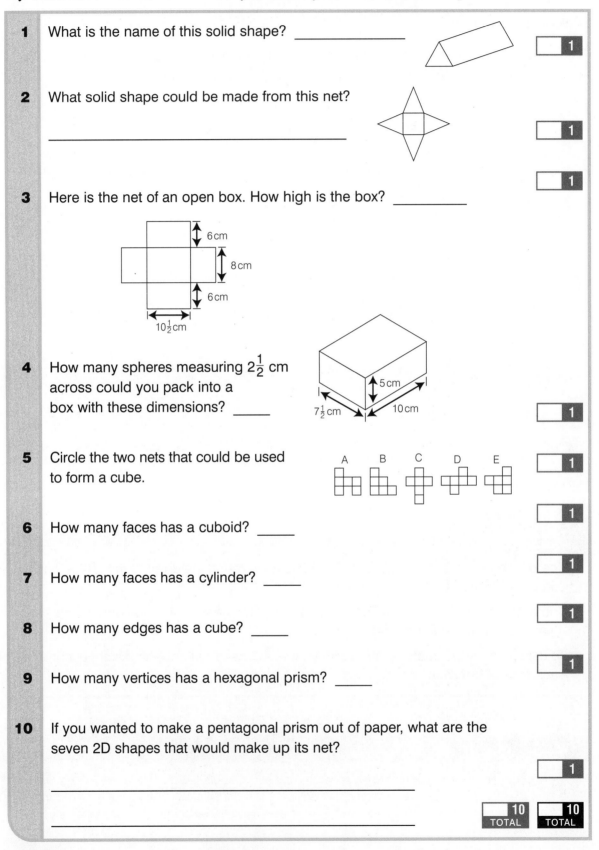

1 What is the name of this solid shape? _____   `1`

2 What solid shape could be made from this net?

_____   `1`

3 Here is the net of an open box. How high is the box? _____   `1`

6 cm

8 cm

6 cm

10½ cm

4 How many spheres measuring 2½ cm across could you pack into a box with these dimensions? _____

5 cm

7½ cm   10 cm   `1`

5 Circle the two nets that could be used to form a cube.

A   B   C   D   E   `1`

6 How many faces has a cuboid? _____   `1`

7 How many faces has a cylinder? _____   `1`

8 How many edges has a cube? _____   `1`

9 How many vertices has a hexagonal prism? _____   `1`

10 If you wanted to make a pentagonal prism out of paper, what are the seven 2D shapes that would make up its net?   `1`

_____

_____

`10` TOTAL   `10` TOTAL

How did you do?

- Nine or ten correct? Read the **Key Facts** and then go on to topic 22: Volume and capacity.
- Eight or fewer correct? Work through this topic carefully and then retake the test!

Naming 3D shapes

You need to recognise and be able to name these 3D shapes:

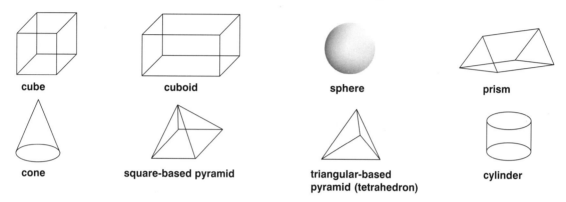

cube	cuboid	sphere	prism
cone	square-based pyramid	triangular-based pyramid (tetrahedron)	cylinder

Prisms have the same shape at both ends with rectangles or squares joining the two ends together. Prisms are named according to their end shape:

triangular prism   pentagonal prism   hexagonal prism

Nets

A net is what you would draw, cut out and fold to make a 3D shape. To work out from a diagram whether a net will make a shape, you have to imagine cutting it out and folding it into the shape.

There are many ways of making the net of a cube. Here are two ways:

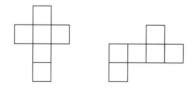

Now it's your turn!

There are 11 different nets of a cube in total. Try to work out the other 9 on squared paper! Cut them out and check that they can be made into cubes.

Now it's your turn!

Look out for solid 3D shapes and try to name them. Make lists of examples in your notebook. Here are some to get you started:

Cone: traffic cone

Cube: a die

Cuboid: a wardrobe

Sphere: a marble

Faces, edges and vertices

The **faces** of a solid 3D shape are the flat parts.

The **edges** of a solid 3D shape are where two faces meet.

The **vertices** of a solid 3D shape are the points or corners.

The plural of **vertex** is **vertices**.

Look back at the diagrams of the 3D shapes on p. 77.

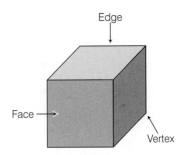

- How many faces has a square-based pyramid?
- How many edges has a cuboid?
- How many vertices has a sphere?

PARENT TIP

Use all shapes and sizes of 3D food packaging to test your child's knowledge of 3D shape names. Ask him or her to count the number of faces, edges and vertices. There are also many maths model-making books available which might be fun to try with your child.

㉒ Volume and capacity

Try this test to find out how much you already know about volume and capacity.

1 What is the volume of this shape? Give the unit of measurement.

_____

4 cm
6 cm
2 cm

1

2 Find the volume of this shape. Give the unit of measurement.

_____

3 m
2 m
5 m

1

3 What is the volume of this shape if one of the cuboids that makes it up has a volume of 9 cubic centimetres?

_____

1

4 The volume of a box is 3600 cm³. If its length is 30 cm and it is 12 cm wide, what is its height?

_____

1

5 How many cubes make up this solid shape?

_____

1

6 This container holds 2 litres of water. How much water is there at the level marked A?

_____

2 l
A → 1 l

1

7 How many millilitres are there in 2.3 litres? _____ `1`

8 One bottle holds 1.7 litres. How many millilitres are there in another bottle that holds twice as much? `1`

_____

9 Granny's teapot holds just enough tea for four cups. Circle the most likely capacity of the teapot: 2 litres, 800 ml, 4 litres, 300 ml, 0.6 litres `1`

10 Three identical bottles will hold 650 ml each. If they are filled up from a 2 l bottle of lemonade, how much will be left in the larger bottle? `1`

_____

`10 TOTAL` `10 TOTAL`

How did you do?
- Nine or ten correct? Read the **Key Facts** and then go on to topic 23: Transformations: coordinates, reflection, rotation and translation.
- Eight or fewer correct? Work through this topic carefully and then retake the test!

Volume

The volume of a solid 3D object is the amount of space it takes up. To find the volume of a cube or cuboid, multiply together the three dimensions: length, breadth and height (l + b + h).

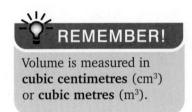

For example the dimensions of this cuboid are:

l = 4 cm
b = 3 cm
h = 2 cm

$4 \times 3 \times 2 = 24$ cm³. The volume of this shape is 24 cm³

To find the volume of an irregular solid object, split it up into cubes or cuboids and find their separate volumes. Then add up the volumes.

1. Look at this irregular solid object:

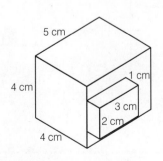

2. It can be split into two separate cuboids:

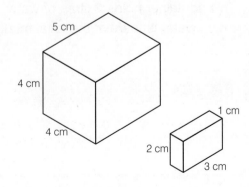

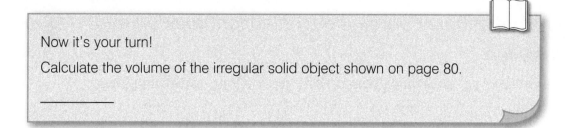

Now it's your turn!

Calculate the volume of the irregular solid object shown on page 80.

_____

Capacity

The **capacity** of a container is how much water or other liquid it will hold. Capacity can be measured in **litres** (l) and/or **millilitres** (ml).

For example, the amount 900 ml can also be written as 0.9 litre. The amount 1400 ml can also be written as 1 l 400 or 1.4 l.

One litre is just under two pints and is the amount in a standard carton of juice; it will give you four large glasses of juice.

REMEMBER!

1 litre = 1000 millilitres

A teacup holds about 200 ml; a mug holds about 300 ml.

1 Write these capacities using just litres.

3100 ml _____   2200 ml _____   5800 ml _____

2 Write these capacities using just millilitres

7.3 litres _____   1.1 litres _____   6.7 litres _____

KEY FACTS

- Volume is the amount of space an object takes up and is measured in **cubic centimetres (cm³)** or **cubic metres (m³)**.

- Volume of a cube/cuboid = **length** × **breadth** × **height** ($l \times b \times h$).

- Capacity is the amount of water a container will hold and is measured in **litres (l)** and/or **millilitres (ml)**.

✔ PARENT TIP

Helping with cooking and baking are practical activities that can help visualise capacities. Comparing the capacity of a range of bathroom or kitchen containers or bottles will also strengthen your child's understanding.

23 *Transformations: coordinates, reflection, rotation and translation*

Try this test to find out how much you already know about transformations.

1 Plot the vertices (2, −2), (4, 4) and (2, 5) on the grid and then join up the vertices.

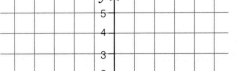

2 Reflect the shape you made in question 1 in the line $x = 0$.

3 Write its new coordinates.

(____, ____), (____, ____),

(____, ____)

4 Translate the shape you made in question 2 one square to the right and two squares down.

5 Write its new coordinates. (____,____), (____,____), (____,____)

6 Plot these points and join them in order. (4, 4), (8, 6) (8, 10), (4, 8)
What have you made? _____

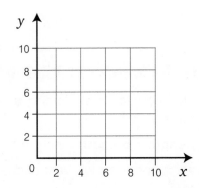

7 Rotate the shape you made in question 6 90° clockwise around point (4, 4).

8 Write its new coordinates. (____,____), (____,____), (____,____)

9 Give the coordinates of point X.

(_____ , _____)

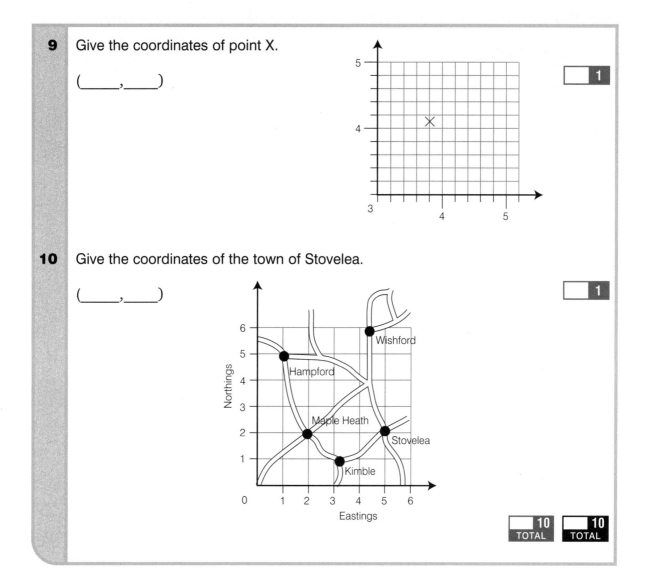

10 Give the coordinates of the town of Stovelea.

(_____ , _____)

10 TOTAL   10 TOTAL

How did you do?
- Nine or ten correct? Read the **Key Facts** and then go on to topic 24: Symmetry.
- Eight or fewer correct? Work through this topic carefully and then retake the test!

Coordinates

In questions about transformations, the points of shapes are given as **coordinates**, such as **(3, 6)**. You may have to plot the shape on the *x*- and *y*- axes yourself.

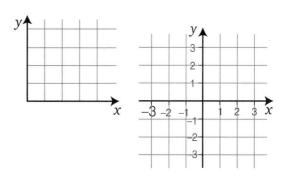

The first number in a pair of coordinates is always the *x* amount and you have to go **along** the *x*-axis.

The second number in a pair of coordinates is always the *y* amount and you have to go **up or down** the *y*-axis.

REMEMBER!

Try remembering that you go 'along the hall first (*x*-axis), and then up the stairs (*y*-axis)' when giving a pair of coordinates.

Reflection, rotation and translation

- **Reflection** means reflecting a shape in a given mirror line.
- **Rotation** means swivelling a shape round a given point or centre of rotation. An object can be rotated **clockwise**, like the hands of a clock, or **anticlockwise**, the opposite way from the hands of a clock.

clockwise   **anticlockwise**

- **Translation** means moving a shape along and up or down a given number of squares.

Look at this example:

1 Plot these coordinates on the grid: (–2, 2), (–2, 4), (–5, 2) and join them together (shape A).

2 Reflect the shape along the line *y* = 1 (shape B).

3 Rotate the original shape 180° clockwise about the point (0, 0) (shape C).

4 Translate shape C 1 square left and 4 squares down (shape D).

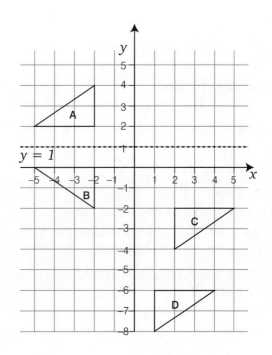

Now it's your turn!

1 Plot these coordinates on the grid: (4, 1), (5, 1), (5, 4) and join them together.

2 Reflect the shape along the line $y = 0$.

3 Rotate the original shape 90° anticlockwise about the point (4, 1).

4 Translate the original shape 4 squares left and 4 squares down.

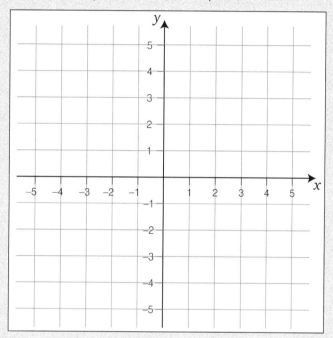

KEY FACTS

- **Coordinates** tell you a specific point on a grid.

- The value on the x-axis must always be given **before** the value on the y-axis: (x, y).

- **Reflection** means reflecting a shape in a mirror line.

- **Rotation** means turning a shape round a point or centre of rotation.

- **Clockwise** is in the same direction as the hands of a clock, **anticlockwise** is the opposite direction.

- **Translation** means moving a shape along and up or down.

✅ PARENT TIP

Draw half a shape (such as a kite, a face, a star, etc.) and ask your child to guess what the full shape will be. Show your child how to use a mirror along the line of reflection to see if his or her guess was correct. You could also use tracing paper to check where a shape should be after a rotation.

㉔ Symmetry

Try this test to find out how much you already know about symmetry.

Look at these shapes.

A   B   C   D   E

Which shape has:

1 one line of symmetry? _____   1

2 two lines of symmetry? _____   1

3 no lines of symmetry? _____   1

4 Complete this figure. The dotted line is a line of symmetry.   1

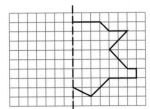

5 How many lines of symmetry has a regular hexagon? _____   1

6 Show all the lines of symmetry of this shape by drawing dotted lines.   1

7 What is the order of rotational symmetry of this shape?

_____   1

Look at these shapes.

A   B   C   D   E

Which shape has order of rotational symmetry:

8 5? _____   1

9 1? _____   1

      1

10 4? _____

10 TOTAL   10 TOTAL

How did you do?

○ Nine or ten correct? Read the **Key Facts** and then go on to topic 25: Metric and imperial units of measurement.

○ Eight or fewer correct? Work through this topic carefully and then retake the test!

Line symmetry

A shape is said to be **symmetrical** when it can be divided into two equal, mirror images by a **line of symmetry**. Shapes can have more than one line of symmetry. Lines of symmetry are usually shown as dotted lines on a diagram:

Sometimes a line of symmetry is shown next to a shape and not on it at all. It allows the shape to be reflected symmetrically. The distances between the points or vertices of the shape and the line of symmetry must be the same for both the shape and its reflected image:

REMEMBER!

Folding is a good way to check if a line is a line of symmetry. The two sides must map onto each other exactly.

Rotational symmetry

Rotational symmetry is when you turn a shape round a point or centre to see how often it maps onto, or fits exactly on top of, itself. The number of times it does this is its **order of symmetry**.

This star has order of symmetry 5 because it maps onto itself 5 times before arriving back at where it started.

✓ **PARENT TIP**

Remind your child that he or she can use a mirror to check a shape for lines of symmetry and tracing paper to test whether or not a shape has rotational symmetry.

Try drawing a range of different shapes in your notebook and then use a mirror to see if they have lines of symmetry. Remember to check if a shape has more than one!

KEY FACTS

● A shape is said to be **symmetrical** when it can be split into two equal, mirror images by a **line of symmetry**.

● Shapes can have more than one line of symmetry.

● A shape is described as having **rotational symmetry** if, when you turn it round, it maps onto itself exactly.

● The number of times a shape maps onto itself is its **order of symmetry**.

Measurement

㉕ Metric and imperial units of measurement

Try this test to find out how much you already know about metric and imperial units of measurement.

---

1 2 m = _____ cm | 1 |

2 3.6 litres = _____ ml | 1 |

3 Which is heavier: 12 kg of potatoes or 12 lb of potatoes? _____ | 1 |

4 Which is shorter: 20 miles or 20 km? _____ | 1 |

5 Is 3 litres or 3 pints more? _____ | 1 |

6 Circle the most likely metric measurement of the height of a normal door:

   400 cm   1.5 m   0.12 km   200 cm   5000 mm | 1 |

7 Circle the best imperial unit to measure the weight of a small apple:

   lb   oz   stone   tonne | 1 |

8 3.5 metres is about the same as:

   11 feet   1 foot   35 feet   3.5 feet   8 feet

   Circle the answer. | 1 |

9 A jug holding 2 litres would hold about _____ pints of water. | 1 |

10 A stone is equal to 14 lb and 1 lb is equal to 454 g.

   If Jack weighs 5 stone, how many kg is that to the nearest kg? _____ | 1 |

| 10 TOTAL | | 10 TOTAL |

How did you do?
- Nine or ten correct? Read the **Key Facts** and then go on to topic 26: Reading scales.
- Eight or fewer correct? Work through this topic carefully and then retake the test!

Metric measurements

All metric units of measurement use tens, hundreds and thousands and are simpler to use than imperial units. Here are some details of metric units used to measure length, weight and capacity:

Length:

Metric equivalents	Examples
1 km (kilometre) = 1000 m (metres)	Kilometres are used to measure large distances between villages, towns and cities.
1 m = 100 cm (centimetres)	1 m is the length of a **metre ruler** (look for one at school!).
1 cm = 10 mm (millimetres)	1 cm is about the width of your **fingertip**. 1 mm is the width of a large **full stop**.

Weight:

1 t (tonne) = 1000 kg (kilograms)	1 **tonne** is about the weight of a **small car**.
1 kg = 1000 g (grams)	1 kg is the weight of a **bag of sugar**.
1 g = 1000 mg (milligrams)	1 g is the weight of a **paper clip**. Ingredients in medicines are often measured in milligrams.

Capacity:

1 l (litre) = 1000 ml (millilitres)	1 l is the capacity of a standard **fruit juice carton**. 500 ml is the capacity of a standard **washing-up liquid bottle**. 330 ml is the capacity of a standard **drink can**. 5 ml is the capacity of a **teaspoon**.

Imperial measurements

Imperial units of measurement were used before metric ones replaced them. Imperial measurements continue to be used, particularly on road signs giving distances in miles. It is therefore important for you to know them and their equivalent metric amounts.

Length:

Imperial equivalents	Metric examples
1 mile = 1760 yards	Almost 2 km.
1 yard (yd) = 3 feet	Just under 1 metre.
1 foot (ft) = 12 inches **REMEMBER!** ≈ means 'approximately equal to'.	The length of a 30 cm ruler. The height of a tall man is about 6 ft or just under 2 m. 1 inch ≈ 2.5 cm

Weight:

1 stone = 14 pounds	Just over 6 kg.
1 pound (lb) = 16 ounces (oz)	The amount of honey in a jar – almost 500 g. 1 oz ≈ 25 g (the weight of three £1 coins).

Capacity:

1 gallon = 8 pints	≈ 4 l 1 pint ≈ $\frac{1}{2}$ litre (Think of a pint of milk.)

It is important for you to know what these metric and imperial measurements look or feel like.

Now it's your turn!

Estimate the weight and then weigh each of 10 different packets of food and make a list to compare these estimates with the actual weights.

Be sure to include one of each of the following in the selection of packets: 1 kg, 500 g, 250 g.

The same activity can be carried out for 10 different capacity containers, including 1 litre, 500 ml and 250 ml.

- There are **metric** and **imperial** units of measurement.

- Metric units of measurement are all based on **tens**, **hundreds** and **thousands**:

  1 km = 1000 m
  1 m = 100 cm
  1 cm = 10 mm
  1 tonne = 1000 kg
  1 kg = 1000 g
  1 g = 1000 mg
  1 litre = 1000 ml

- Imperial units of measurement include **miles**, **stones** and **pints**:

  1 mile = 1760 yards
  1 yard (yd) = 3 feet
  1 foot (ft) = 12 inches
  1 stone = 14 pounds
  1 pound (lb) = 16 ounces (oz)
  1 gallon = 8 pints

- These **approximate equivalences** show the relationships between metric and imperial measures:

  1 ounce (oz) ≈ 25 g
  1 pint ≈ $\frac{1}{2}$ litre

26 Reading scales

Try this test to find out how much you already know about reading scales.

1 What is the mass shown by pointer A in kilograms and grams?

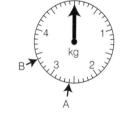

_____

| | 1 |

2 How many grams must be added to the amount marked by pointer B to make 4 kg?

_____

| | 1 |

3 The line AB is drawn to a scale of 1 cm to 1 m.

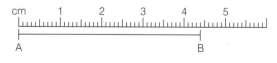

Write in metres and centimetres the length represented by AB.

_____

| | 1 |

4 At the supermarket you put some potatoes on the scale.

What will the potatoes cost if the price is 36p per kilogram?

_____   [1]

5 When Kim weighs herself, the dial on the scales points to here:

What is Kim's weight in kilograms and grams? _____   [1]

6 How many more grams of grass seed do you have to
buy to make the amount up to 700 g?

_____   [1]

7 You decide you only need to buy 335 g of grass seed.

How many grams need to be removed? _____   [1]

8 A map is drawn to a scale of 1 : 2000.
What distance in metres would be represented by 6 cm on the map?

_____   [1]

9 What distance in metres would be represented by 13 cm on the map?

_____   [1]

10 How much water is there in this measuring beaker? _____   [1]

	10
	TOTAL

	10
	TOTAL

How did you do?

- Nine or ten correct? Read the **Key Facts** and then go on to topic 27: Time and timetables.
- Eight or fewer correct? Work through this topic carefully and then retake the test!

Types of scales

A scale can be read in a straight line like a ruler or round like a dial.

It is very important to look carefully for the unit of measurement given on a scale. The jug says 1 litre at the top, and the markings below it represent 10 and 100 millilitres. The round dial says kg, meaning kilograms; therefore the smaller divisions represent 100 grams.

Next it is important to work out what one division on a scale is worth. Here are some 1-litre jugs, each with different division lines marked on them:

REMEMBER!

1 l = 1000 ml
1 kg = 1000 g

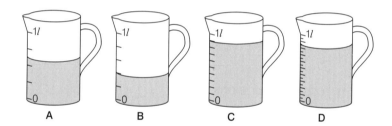

A   B   C   D

a 1000 ml ÷ 4 equal size sections = 250 ml per section.

b 1000 ml ÷ 5 equal size sections = 200 ml per section.

c 1000 ml ÷ 10 equal size sections = 100 ml per section.

d 1000 ml ÷ 20 equal size sections = 50 ml per section.

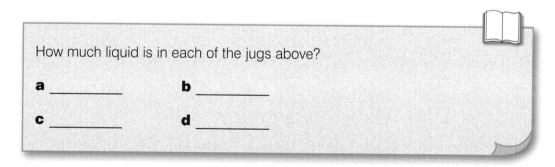

How much liquid is in each of the jugs above?

a _____   **b** _____

c _____   **d** _____

- A **scale** can be read in a straight line like a ruler or round like a dial.
- Look for the **units of measurement** marked on a scale or dial.
- Calculate what each **division line** is worth on any scale you are given.

✓ PARENT TIP

Encourage your child to help measure out ingredients in the kitchen using measuring jugs and non-digital scales. Remind your child that his or her eye must be at the same height as the liquid level in a jug to read the amount accurately. Talk about other types of scales together, e.g. bathroom scales, maps, a fuel gauge in the car, etc.

(27) *Time and timetables*

Try this test to find out how much you already know about time and timetables.

1 `20:35`

Write this 24-hour clock time using a.m. or p.m. _____ ☐ 1

2 Change 1.40 p.m. to a 24-hour clock time: _____ ☐ 1

3 40 minutes + 38 minutes + _____ = 2 hours. ☐ 1

4 200 minutes is _____ hours _____ minutes. ☐ 1

5 The Masons' holiday is from 16 January until 13 February, including both dates.

How many days is this? _____ ☐ 1

6 Use this part of a calendar to find the date of the third Monday in June. ☐ 1

_____

		June				
M	**T**	**W**	**Th**	**F**	**Sa**	**Su**
			1	2	3	4
5	6	7	8	9	10	11
12	13	14	15	16		

7 What is the time three-quarters of an hour before 01.35? _____ [1]

8 How many minutes are there from 11.37 p.m. on Thursday until 1.13 a.m. on Friday? [1]

_____

[1]

9 How many hours are there in $2\frac{1}{2}$ days? _____

10 Here is part of a train timetable. Fill in the time at which train B will arrive at Langford if it takes the same amount of time as train A. You will need to work out all of the times to find the answer.

	Train A arrives at	Train B arrives at
Stokesby	06.45	07.30
Linton	07.08	
Doole	07.36	
Pimwich	08.12	
Langford	08.19	
Pagnell	08.24	

[1]

10 TOTAL   10 TOTAL

How did you do?
- Nine or ten correct? Read the **Key Facts** and then look through the glossary to check you know all of the key 11+ Maths terms.
- Eight or fewer correct? Work through this topic carefully and then retake the test!

Telling the time

Telling the time is an essential skill. You need to be able to tell the time in words using a clock with hands (**analogue** time) and write a time in figures (**digital** time).

The 12-hour clock is based on the day having two sets of 12 hours. To make the difference clear between the times, **a.m.** (morning) or **p.m.** (afternoon) is written after the time. So, 9.00 a.m. is 9 o'clock in the morning and 9.00 p.m. is 9 o'clock in the evening.

The 24-hour clock is shown on some digital clocks. It continues after 12.00 at lunchtime like this: 13.00, 14.00, and so on, with 13.00 being 1 o'clock and 14.00 being 2 o'clock. So, 16.00 is 4 o'clock in the afternoon.

> **REMEMBER!**
> Midnight in the 24-hour clock is zero hours: 00.00.

24-hour clock times always have four digits and therefore have a '0' written before the hours 1 to 9 in the morning: 03.25.

Months

It is important to know how many days are in each month of the year for some questions. This mnemonic can help you to remember how long each month lasts:

> 30 days have September, April, June and November
> All the rest have 31
> Except February alone
> Which has 28 days clear
> And 29 in each leap year.

Timetables

Timetables generally use the 24-hour clock.

To find the difference between two times, it can be useful to count the whole hours first and then count the minutes.

Look at this example:

If a bus leaves at 09.16 and arrives at its destination at 16.03, how long did the journey take?

$$09.16 \longrightarrow 15.16 = 6 \text{ hours}$$

$$15.16 \longrightarrow 16.03 = 47 \text{ minutes}$$

The journey took 6 hours 47 minutes.

Now it's your turn!

If a train leaves at 10.27 and arrives at its destination at 15.09, how long did the journey take? _____

✔ **PARENT TIP**

Ask your child to use a timetable to work out how long a bus or train journey that you will be going on will take. It can also be helpful to ask children questions such as "How many days is it until we…?" followed by "What date will that be?" Or even, "How long is it until bedtime?!"

KEY FACTS

- The **12-hour clock** uses the hours 1 to 12 twice in one day. Use **a.m.** to show a time in the morning and **p.m.** to show a time in the afternoon or evening.

- The **24-hour clock** uses the hours 0.00 to 24.00, with 0.00 being midnight and 12.00 being midday. A.m. and p.m. are not used with 24-hour times.

- Know how many days there are in each month of the year (see the mnemonic months rhyme).

- **Timetables** generally use the 24-hour clock.

C: How do you prepare for the exam?

① What next?

You've worked through this book. Now test yourself!

If you used the central pull-out test before reading this book, have another go at it now and see how you have improved. Please visit www.bond11plus.co.uk and follow the Free Resources link to download another free copy. For more practice, and to put your skills to the test, work through the range of books and test papers in the *Bond 11+ Maths* range.

Mark your answers with an adult. Talk about the questions you got wrong or found hard to understand. Read the sections in this book again to help brush up on things you are still not sure about.

② Build confidence with practice

It is a good idea to go over examples of things that might come up in an 11+ Maths exam well before the date. A useful way to do this is to try some maths tests that are similar to the exam you will be doing. The *Bond* papers used regularly, perhaps once a fortnight during Year 5 and Year 6 term-time weeks and once a week during the holidays, will provide useful, graded practice that will build your confidence and show you how well you cope with doing tests of this kind.

✔ **PARENT TIP**

For more advice on practice routines and useful techniques, read The Parents' Guide to the 11+. See inside cover for more details.

③ Time yourself

If you are just starting to prepare yourself, you may find it helpful to whizz through your first few *Bond Assessment Papers in Maths* untimed. This will help you to familiarise yourself with the types of questions and tasks you will face in the exam. Note down your scores (you could use the progress grids at the back of the *Bond Assessment Papers*) and be sure to go over all the questions you found difficult until you understand them. After that, though, it is very important to give yourself a set time, just as you will have in the exam, so that you can practise pacing yourself and aiming to complete everything in the given time.

✔ **PARENT TIP**

Remember to be encouraging and positive about what your child produces! If there are mistakes or some parts still cause difficulty, that's quite natural; no one's perfect!

④ Revise strategies and techniques

It is also worth thinking about exam strategies and techniques. For many children, 11+ exams are the first exams they do in their lives, and they get very nervous at the thought of them. So do their parents! There are lots of hints on strategies and techniques in this book. Flick through them and talk about them to remind yourself. It may be a good idea to make a reminder list of things to particularly look out for in the exam.

It is very important to remember that everyone is different. You will have your own way of coping and of doing things which may be quite different from the way other people work. If you have worked through this book, you will have a good idea of your own strengths and weaknesses, the things you find easy or difficult. You will have developed your own strategies and techniques in tests and in your learning.

⑤ The exam day itself

"I'm so nervous…"

Of course you may be nervous, but actually, when it comes to the day, many people find they can enjoy their exams, as long as they feel confident and well prepared. After all, you will have done all the practice; now it's your chance to show what you can do!

Just before the exam

Here are some useful things to remember before the exam day arrives:

Checklist

- ✓ Don't worry about feeling a bit nervous; that's natural. Most children will feel anxious. Talk about your feelings and try to relax.
- ✓ Plan something fun to do after the exam is over.
- ✓ Try to have a good night's sleep.

On the day

Checklist

- ✓ Eat a healthy breakfast and have something to drink.
- ✓ Get to the place where the exam is happening in plenty of time.
- ✓ Find out where the toilets are and go if you can before the exam starts.

In the exam room

There should be no distractions during the exam because everyone is in the same boat as you and there will be at least one adult making sure that everything runs smoothly. The adult will also tell you when to start, when to stop and will keep an eye on you all so that, for instance, there is no cheating.

Here are some useful strategies and techniques to remember once you are in the exam room:

Checklist

✓ **Keep calm.** If you get butterflies or feel anxious, sit up straight, make sure your shoulders are not hunched and take some deep breaths. This allows plenty of oxygen to get to your brain, which needs it!

✓ **Think positive.** You've done all the hard work preparing. Now enjoy yourself!

✓ **Find the clock.** Make sure you know where it is before you start, so you can do a time-check during the exam.

✓ **Read the question.** Not doing so is the most common mistake and easy to do something about.

✓ **Write careful answers.** Again, most mistakes are careless ones or 'kick yourself' mistakes.

✓ **Show what you know.** This is your big moment and what you've practised for. Try to enjoy showing what you have learnt.

✓ **If you can't do a question, don't panic:** have a go. Write something, and then put a mark in the margin, showing that you need to have another look if you have time at the end. Remember: a blank scores zero; a good guess may well be right.

✓ **Leave time to check.** Remember to leave a few minutes to check through your answers and make sure they make sense.

✓ **Do your best:** you can't do better than that!

GOOD LUCK!

Glossary

24-hour clock – the 24-hour clock uses the hours 0.00 to 24.00, with 0.00 being midnight and 12.00 being midday.

acute angle – an angle of less than 90°.

acute-angled triangle – this has three acute angles.

algebra – the part of maths that deals with finding missing numbers in equations.

a.m. – the time between midnight and midday.

analogue time – the time written in words using a clock with hands.

angle – measured in degrees, an angle tells us how far something turns or rotates.

arc – a part of the circumference of a circle.

area – how much space there is inside a 2D shape, measured in square units, e.g. cm², m², km².

average – see mean.

axis (plural 'axes') – a graph has two lines called axes, the x-axis and y-axis, which join or intersect.

bearing – an angle between the direction north and the direction in which something is travelling.

capacity – how much liquid a container will hold, measured in litres (l) or millilitres (ml).

circumference – the distance around a circle.

concentric circles – circles that share the same centre point but have a different radius.

consecutive numbers – numbers that follow on in order.

coordinates – these indicate the points, e.g. (3, 4), on x- and y-axes. The first number is always the x amount; the second number is always the y amount.

cube number – a number that is multiplied by itself twice.

cuboid – a 3D shape which has six rectangular faces.

data – collections of information.

decimal fraction – tenths, hundredths, thousandths, etc. shown as digits after a decimal point.

denominator – the bottom part of a fraction; it tells you how many equal parts the whole has been divided into.

diameter – the distance straight across a circle, going through the centre.

digit – a single number from 0 to 9.

digital time – the time written in numbers, as you would see on a digital clock.

divisible – a number is divisible by a smaller number if the smaller number divides exactly into the larger number.

edge – the line where two faces of a solid 3D shape meet.

equation – a number sentence where one thing is equal to something else.

equilateral triangle – this has three equal sides and three equal angles.

equivalent fractions – fractions that are equal to one another.

estimate – make a sensible guess at an answer.

face – the flat part of a solid 3D shape.

factor – a whole number that will divide exactly into another number.

fraction – a part of a whole.

graph – a visual way of displaying data; it can have bars, lines or pictures representing the data.

highest common factor (HCF) – The HCF of a set of numbers is the largest number that is a factor of all numbers in the set.

horizontal – straight across.

hundredth – one whole divided into 100 equal parts.

improper fraction – a top-heavy fraction where the numerator is larger than the denominator.

index – the number of times a number is multiplied by itself, e.g. $2 \times 2 \times 2 = 2^3$ has an index of 3.

integer – a whole number.

inverse – the opposite of something.

isosceles triangle – this has two equal sides and two equal angles.

lowest common multiple (LCM) – the LCM of a set of numbers is the smallest number that is a multiple of all numbers in the set.

mean – the number found by adding together all of the numbers in a set and dividing by how many numbers there are in the set.

median – the middle number in a set when the numbers are put in order of size.

mixed number – a mixture of a whole number and a fraction.

mode – the number in a set of data that comes up most often.

multiple – a multiple of a number is the answer when it is multiplied by another number.

negative number – a number that is less than zero.

net – what you would draw, cut out and fold to make a 3D shape.

numerator – the top part of a fraction; it tells you how many equal parts you are interested in.

obtuse angle – an angle greater than 90° but less than 180°.

obtuse-angled triangle – this has one obtuse angle.

order of symmetry – the number of times a shape maps exactly onto itself when turned round a point.

parallel – lines that are parallel never meet but run the same distance apart from each other for their entire length; they are not necessarily straight.

percentage – out of 100.

perimeter – the total distance around the edge of a 2D shape.

perpendicular – two lines are perpendicular if they are at right angles to each other.

pie chart – a circle divided into sections to show how something is shared into groups.

p.m. – the time between midday and midnight.

polygon – a 2D shape with three or more straight sides.

positive number – a number that is more than zero.

prime factor – the prime factor of a number is the prime number which can be multiplied together to make that number.

prime number – a prime number has only two factors: one and the number itself.

prism – a 3D shape with the same shape at each end and rectangles or squares joining the two ends together.

probability – the chance or possibility of something happening, usually written as a fraction.

proportion – the share of the total amount when you divide up that amount using a given ratio.

quadrilateral – a four-sided, 2D shape.

quotient – the number you get when you divide one number by another.

radius – the distance from the centre of a circle to the circumference; half the diameter.

range – the range of a set of numbers is the difference between the smallest number and the largest number.

ratio – a ratio is used to compare two or more numbers or quantities and is usually expressed with a colon between the numbers.

reflection – reflecting a shape in a given mirror line.

reflex angle – an angle greater than 180°.

remainder – the number left over when one number doesn't divide exactly into another.

right angle – an angle of 90° (think of the corner of a piece of paper).

right-angled triangle – this has one right angle.

Roman numerals – capital letters, once used by Romans, which represent numbers.

rotation – turning a shape around a given point or centre of rotation, either clockwise or anticlockwise.

rotational symmetry – this is when you turn a shape round a point or centre to see how often it maps onto, or fits exactly on top of, itself.

scalene triangle – this has no equal sides and no equal angles.

semicircle – half a circle.

square-based pyramid – a 3D shape with a square base whose other edges meet at a point.

square number – a number that is multiplied by itself.

square root – the square root of a number is the number you multiply by itself to make that number.

symmetry – a shape has symmetry when it can be divided into two equal, mirror images.

tenth – one whole divided into 10 equal parts.

tetrahedron – see triangular-based pyramid.

thousandth – one whole divided into 1000 equal parts.

translation – moving a shape right or left a given number of squares and up or down a given number of squares.

triangular-based pyramid – a 3D shape with a triangular base whose other edges meet at a point.

triangular number – a number that can be arranged as a triangle using, for example, dots.

Venn diagram – a diagram in which data is organised into overlapping circles.

vertex (plural 'vertices') – the point or corner of a solid 3D shape.

vertical – straight up or down.

volume – the amount of space a solid 3D object takes up, measured in cm³ or m³.

whole number – a number that does not have any fractions or remainders with it.

Answers
B: The key 11+ Maths topics

Number

(1) Place value

Test (p. 8)

1 18 000
2 0.305
3 73 100
4 100
5 5
6 $x = 3$; $y = 3$ hundredths

7 66 666
8 700
9 8000
10 1.6

Practice box (p. 11)

1 10 – 345 680
  1000 – 346 000
2 tenth – 476.5

100 – 345 700
10 000 – 350 000
hundredth – 476.53

(2) Addition and subtraction problems

Test (p. 11)

1 1321
2 4645
3 962 m
4 60
5 273

6 25
7 £3.66
8 £10.49
9 4751
10 1179

Practice box (p. 13)

10 474

Practice box (p. 13)

1 157
2 598

(3) Multiplication and division problems

Test (p. 14)

1 20
2 £41.70
3 34 650
4 20
5 £4.08

6 7
7 40
8 9000
9 90
10 12

Practice box (p. 15)

14 256 kg

Practice box (p. 16)

21

(4) Mixed or several-step problems

Test (p. 17)

1 £3.65
2 8
3 600 ml
4 23
5 300 grams

6 6.9 kilograms
7 0.27 m
8 £2.80
9 105
10 £4.90

Practice box (p. 19)

166

(5) Factors and multiples

Test (p. 19)

1 32, 40, 48, 56, 64
2 12
3 4, 6, 8
4 1, 2, 3, 4, 6, 8, 12, 16, 24 and 48
5 63, 70, 77 and 84
6 8
7 60
8 7 and 11
9 2, 2, 3 and 3
10 91

Practice box (p. 21)

21: 1, 3, 7 and 21
35: 1, 5, 7 and 35
56: 1, 2, 4, 7, 8, 14, 28 and 56
HCF = 7

Practice box (p. 22)

First five multiples of 12: 12, 24, 36, 48 and 60
LCM = 24

(6) Special numbers

Test (p. 22)

1 +13°C
2 34
3 34
4 7^2
5 125

6 11
7 41, 43 and 47
8 X
9 13, 14 and 15
10 36

Practice box (p. 25)
XX: 20
XXXV: 35
CL: 150

Practice box (p. 26)
1 31
2 118

7 Sequences

Test (p. 26)
1 $6\frac{1}{2}$ 6 9
2 81   7 6
3 73   8 0.625
4 32   9 10
5 16   10 15

Practice box (p. 28)
25, 11

8 Equations and algebra

Test (p. 29)
1 137   6 8
2 11   7 $x = 12$
3 $x = 12; y = 287$ 8 $x = £3.90$
4 45   9 $a = 4$
5 7   10 150

Practice box (p. 30)
$b = 16; y = 5$

Practice box (p. 31)
$y = 11; z = 27, a = 7$

Practice box (p. 30)
$\frac{15}{16}$ 10

9 Function machines

Test (p. 32)
1 63   5 30
2 30   6 28
3 48   7 37
4 87   8 3
9

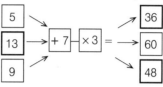
10
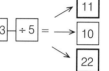

Practice box (p. 34)
83

Fractions and decimals

10 Fractions

Test (p. 35)
1 135   6 28
2 £6.50   7 2
3 20   8 $\frac{2}{5}$
4 $\frac{7}{8}$ $\frac{3}{4}$ $\frac{1}{2}$ $\frac{2}{5}$ $\frac{3}{8}$ $\frac{1}{3}$ $\frac{1}{4}$ 9 $\frac{4}{6}$ $\frac{1}{3}$
5 $3\frac{5}{7}$ 10 $8\frac{3}{5}$

Introduction
Practice box (p. 36)
$\frac{3}{10}$ =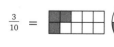

Fractions of numbers
Practice box (p. 43)
9; 35; 14
7; 32; 25

Mixed numbers
Practice box (p. 37)
$6\frac{4}{5}$ =

$4\frac{3}{8}$ =

Improper fractions
Practice box (p. 38)
$1\frac{1}{6}$; $24\frac{1}{4}$

Equivalent fractions
Practice box (p. 38)
$\frac{4}{5}$ = $\frac{8}{10}$ $\frac{12}{15}$ $\frac{16}{20}$

$\frac{3}{8}$ = $\frac{6}{16}$ $\frac{9}{24}$ $\frac{12}{32}$

Practice box (p. 39)
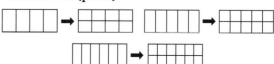

Fraction calculations
Practice box (p. 39)
$1\frac{1}{4}$; $\frac{5}{8}$

Simplifying fractions
Practice box (p. 40)
$\frac{1}{7}$; $\frac{1}{2}$; $\frac{7}{10}$

(11) Decimal fractions
Test (p. 41)
1 3.03 3.3 3.33 3.333 3.42
2 6.3
3 $\frac{21}{25}$ 7 2.1
4 41.391   8 0.27
5 0.008   9 0.6 1
6 1.468   10 12.6

Converting between decimal and vulgar fractions
Practice box (p. 43)
0.35; 0.678; 0.75
0.125; 0.35; 0.8

Practice box (p. 43)
$5\frac{4}{5}$; $11\frac{7}{10}$; $23\frac{3}{500}$

$5\frac{7}{25}$; $7\frac{1}{2}$; $4\frac{3}{25}$

Practice box (p. 44)
3.142, 3.214, 3.241, 3.412, 3.421

Add, subtract, multiply and divide
Practice box (p. 45)
5; 5; 35
16; 20; 20

(12) Percentages
Test (p. 46)
1 40p   6 45%
2 £187.50   7 60%
3 336   8 882
4 24   9 £14 950
5 £28   10 £94

Practice box (p. 47)
306

Practice box (p. 48)
£264.50

(13) Ratio and proportion
Test (p. 49)
1 9   6 £2
2 3 : 2   7 25
3 27   8 £24
4 6   9 39
5 £35   10 8

Practice box (p. 51)
12

Handling data

(14) Organising and comparing information
Test (p. 52)
1 30
2 15 kg
3 11.30 a.m.; 1 km
4 5
5 4
6 13 km/h
7 School B
8 17
9 9
10 31

Practice box (p. 55)
1
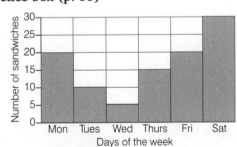

2
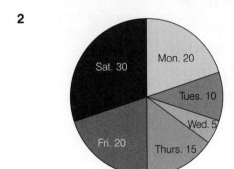

(15) Mean, median, mode and range

Test (p. 56)

1 7	**6** 15
2 124 km	**7** 49
3 81 km/h	**8** 36
4 19	**9** 10 years 11 months
5 10	**10** 160 km

Practice box (p. 57)

Range: 4   Mode: 6   Median: 6   Mean: 6

(16) Probability

Test (p. 58)

1 $\frac{1}{6}$;	**6** $\frac{1}{3}$
2 $\frac{1}{2}$	**7** $\frac{5}{10}$
3 $\frac{1}{52}$	**8** $\frac{3}{7}$
4 $\frac{1}{36}$	**9** $\frac{4}{7}$
5 $\frac{1}{6}$	**10** 0

Practice box (p. 60) $\frac{5}{36}$

Shape and space

(17) 2D shapes: circles, angles and bearings

Test (p. 61)

1 120°	**6** 110°
2 180°	**7** 13 mm
3 60°	**8** Y
4 43°	**9** N
5 38 mm	**10** 5 mm

(18) 2D shapes: triangles

Test (p. 64)

1 55°	**6** 70°
2 Equilateral	**7** E
3 42 cm²	**8** 9 cm²
4 70°	**9** 1
5 Scalene	**10** Acute-angled triangle

Types of triangle
Practice box (p. 66)
180°

Area of a triangle
Practice box (p. 67)

1 6 cm²   **2** 5 cm²   **3** 9 cm²

(19) 2D shapes: quadrilaterals and polygons

Test (p. 68)

1 D

2 A = rhombus   B = parallelogram
C = kite   D = square   E = trapezium

3 50°

4 D
5 B
6

7

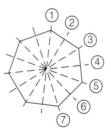

8 130°
9 Heptagon
10 Octagons and squares

Quadrilaterals
Practice box (p. 70)
360°

(20) Perimeter and area

Test (p. 72)

1 12 m	**7** Accept any answer between 130 m² and 150 m²
2 44 m	
3 15	
4 16 cm²	**8** 14 mm
5 48 cm²	**9** 44 m²
6 66 m²	**10** B and D

Practice box (p. 75)

Length = 13 cm   Perimeter = 40 cm

(21) 3D shapes

Test (p. 76)
1 Triangular prism
2 Square-based pyramid
3 6 cm   7 3
4 24   8 12
5 C and D   9 12
6 6   10 Two pentagons
                            and five squares

Nets

Practice box (p. 77)
11 nets of a cube:

(22) Volume and capacity

Test (p. 79)
1 48 cm³   6 800 ml
2 15 m³   7 2300 ml
3 144 cm³   8 3400 ml
4 10 cm   9 800 ml
5 39   10 50 ml

Volume

Practice box (p. 81)
86 cm²

Capacity

Practice box (p. 81)
1 3.1 litres; 2.2 litres; 5.8 litres
2 7300 ml; 1100 ml; 6700 ml

(23) Transformations: coordinates, reflection, rotation and translation

Test (p. 82)
1

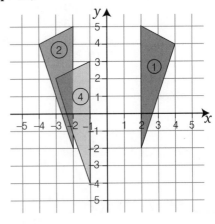

2 See picture above
3 (–2, –2), (–4, 4), (–2, 5)
4 See picture above
5 (–1, –4), (–3, 2), (–1, 3)
6 Rhombus

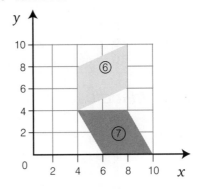

7 See picture above
8 (4, 4), (6, 0), (10, 0) (8, 4)
9 (3.8, 4.1)
10 (5, 2)

Practice box (p. 85)

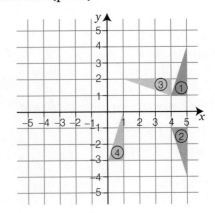

(24) Symmetry

Test (p. 86)

1 C
2 B
3 D
4

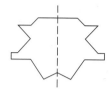

5 6

6

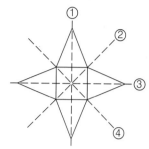

7 3
8 B
9 C
10 A   a

Measurement

(25) Metric and imperial units of measurement

Test (p. 88)

1 200 cm
2 3600 ml
3 12 kg
4 20 km
5 3 l
6 200 cm
7 oz
8 11 feet
9 4 pints
10 32 kg

(26) Reading scales

Test (p. 91)

1 2 kg 600 g
2 600 g
3 4 m 40 cm
4 £1.26
5 46 kg 700 g
6 140 g
7 225 g
8 120 m
9 260 m
10 66 ml

Practice box (p. 93)

a 625 ml
b 400 ml
c 900 ml
d 850 ml

(27) Time and timetables

Test (p. 94)

1 8.35 p.m.
2 13.40
3 42 min
4 3 hours 20 min
5 29
6 19 June
7 00.50
8 96
9 60
10

	Train A arrives at	Train B arrives at
Stokesby	06.45	07.30
Linton	07.08	07.53
Doole	07.36	08.21
Pimwich	08.12	08.57
Langford	08.19	**09.04**
Pagnell	08.24	09.09

09.04

Practice box (p. 96)

4 hours 42 minutes

Standard 11+ maths test (Central pull-out section)

1 20
2 8000
3 2 m 3 cm
4 66°
5 294°
6 8.4 cm
7 72
8 (2, 5.5)
9 (5.5, 3.5)
10 (1, 2.5)
11 (4, 1)
12 15, 18, 20
13 £1500

14 6.10
15 6
16 9
17 3 : 4
18 12
19 52%
20 84
21 £1.70
22 2.47
23 $\frac{7}{8}$
24 5
25 $6 \times 6 \times 6 \times 6 \times 6$
26 $3a = 5b$

27 6
28 4
29 Yes
30 No
31 No
32 No
33 No
34 28 cm
35 $a - 12$
36 90
37 2250
38 $1\frac{19}{25}$

39 $\frac{2}{11}$
40 8
41 20 m
42 13 m^2
43 £104
44 £14.25
45 £5.75
46 £623.75
47 9
48 20
49 04.45
50 1.7 m